Beautiful
BISCUITS

TESSA WHITEHOUSE

First published in November 2016 by B. Dutton Publishing Limited, The Grange, Hones Yard, Farnham, Surrey, GU9 8BB, UK.

Copyright: Tessa Whitehouse 2016

ISBN-13: 978-1-905113-55-2

Publisher: Beverley Dutton

Editor-in-Chief: Jennifer Kelly

Art Director/Designer: Sarah Ryan

Editor: Jenny Weaver

Copy Editors: Frankie New, Adele Duthie

Photography: Robert Goves

PR and Advertising Manager: Natalie Bull

Printed and bound in Slovenia by arrangement with Associated Agencies, Oxford

Disclaimer

The Author and Publisher have made every effort to ensure that the contents of this book, if followed carefully, will not cause harm or injury or pose any danger. Please note that any inedible used in the projects in this book must be removed before the biscuits are eaten. Similarly, any equipment and substances not approved for contact with food must not come into contact with any biscuit or decoration that is to be eaten. Neither the Author nor the Publisher can be held responsible for errors or omissions and cannot accept liability for injury, damage or loss to persons or property, however it may arise, as a result of acting upon guidelines and information printed in this book.

How to make impressive iced cookies for special occasions

Enjoy!
Teri>

Beautiful
BISCUITS

Acknowledgements

Thank you to my long-suffering husband, Rob, who has put up with months of baking smells with only limited opportunities for tasters and the many occasions on which he found yet another stack of biscuit dough chilling in our fridge.

To friends and family for patiently supporting me while I have been biscuit obsessed.

And finally to Beverley and all those at B. Dutton Publishing who invited me to do this book and who have supported me so ably through the process.

Introduction

Decorated biscuits make great treats, gifts and favours. Decoration can range from the very simple to the extravagant and they are a perennial favourite with avid bakers because they are so accessible to everyone. My approach is to start with a tasty biscuit and think of fun designs that look impressive but aren't too time consuming to create.

I have baked and decorated ever since I can remember, starting with Christmas cakes made with my grandmother. I developed my skills over time through reading books but they really took off when Squires Kitchen became my local sugarcraft shop. I attended several demonstrations and courses and since then have made sugarcraft a second career. My true passion is royal icing – I just love what can be achieved using this versatile sugar medium, from coating a biscuit through to making the most intricate and delicate decorations.

You can make all of the iced biscuit projects in this book using one of the recipes given at the start then decorate them following the simple step-by-step instructions and photographs. As well as creating some fun and colourful designs you will learn some clever icing techniques, so if the mood takes you, you can use your imagination to create your very own works of biscuit art!

Contents

Essential Edibles and Equipment

1   Airtight containers (not pictured)

2   Art-Ice Cookie Icing Mix (SK)

3   Baking parchment

4   Baking sheets/trays

5   Biscuit cutters (see note on page 11)

6   Cellophane

7   Craft knife

8   Cocktail sticks

9   Desk lamp with 40W bulb

10 Digital weighing scales (not pictured)

11 Disposable piping bags: paper (small and medium),
    plastic (medium)

12 Dust food colours (SK)

13 Fine sieve

14 Food colour pens (SK)

15 Instant Mix Royal Icing: Tuxedo Black and White (SK)

16 Liquid food colours (SK)

17 Masking tape

18 Paintbrushes: nos. 2 and 4 round, no. 10 flat

19 Palette knives: large, small cranked

20 Piping bottles with nozzles

21 Piping nozzles: nos. 1, 1.5, 2, 3 (PME)

22 Rolling pin guide rings (PME)

23 Rolling pins: large and small

24 Round or square cake drums, 15cm or 20.5cm (6" or 8")

25 Scribing tool

26 Small bowls

27 Small measuring jug

28 Small, sharp knife

29 Small, sharp scissors

30 Spatula

31 Stand mixer (not pictured)

32 White vegetable fat (not pictured)

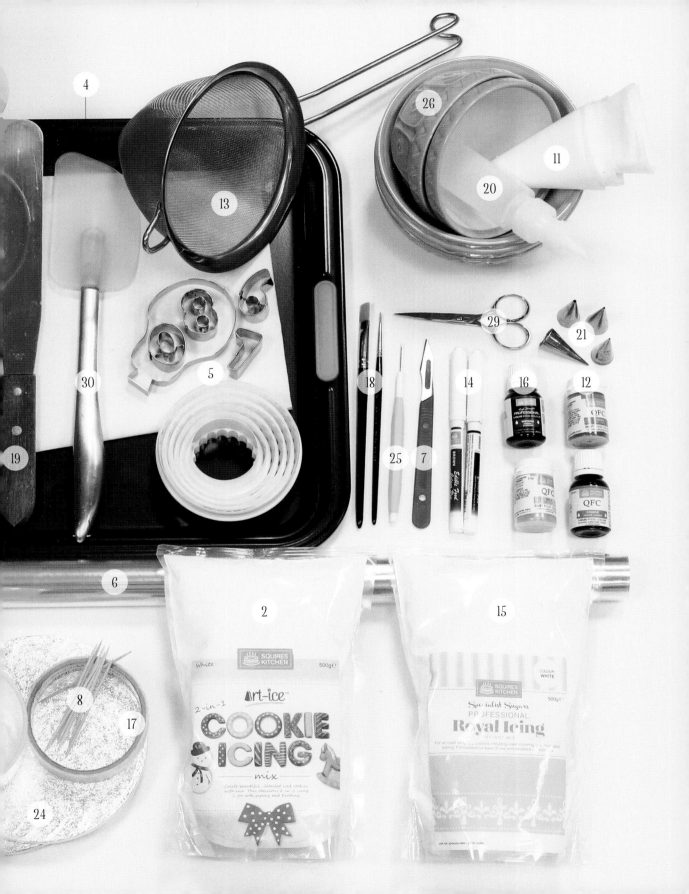

Piping bottles or piping bags?

I have used both icing bottles and disposable paper piping bags throughout this book. I find them useful for slightly different purposes, depending on the biscuit project.

Icing bottles (with nozzle and adaptor): These are good for filling large areas. They are easy to refill if a lot of one colour is to be used and it is quick to change the nozzle size if necessary. It is also easy to see if the icing is starting to separate and needs stirring – simply use a clean chopstick or dowel rod for this.

Bottles must be used with a nozzle, those supplied with the bottle are usually around a no. 2 size.

Bottles are not always easy to control and can be wasteful, so for small areas or detail I would recommend using a piping bag.

Disposable paper piping bags: I use two sizes, medium or small depending on how much icing I need. I use a small piping bag fitted with a nozzle for piping outlines and details and a small or medium piping bag with no nozzle to fill outlined areas with run-out icing: half-fill the bag with icing then cut a small hole in the tip. This method is useful if you are using several run-out colours as it reduces the number of nozzles needed.

The main disadvantage with paper piping bags is that they can go soggy over time, particularly if no nozzle is fitted.

Disposable plastic piping bags: These can be used in place of either piping bottles or paper piping bags. They are easily refillable and can be used with a coupler to make changing nozzle sizes easier.

Plastic piping bags tend to be medium to large in size so are good for large areas but they can also be cut down in size to make them smaller for delicate work. They are best used with piping nozzles as the seam can disrupt the smooth flow of icing from the bag.

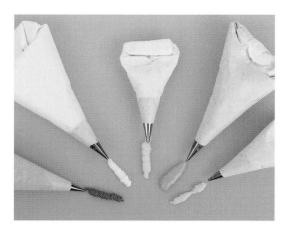

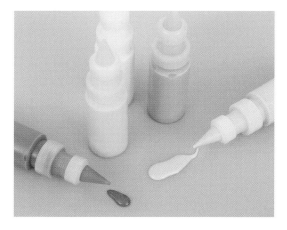

Cutters

Metal cutters tend to cut more cleanly and accurately than plastic ones. However, if they are made from tin plate they are prone to rusting so dry them off fully before packing away; drying in the residual heat of the oven after baking is ideal. Take care not to damage the edges of the cutters you use to make your biscuits – if they become nicked or distorted they will no longer cut cleanly.

TUTOR TIP

Some cutters are made so they can only be used one way, if you want a left- and right-facing biscuit simply flip the raw, cut-out biscuit over when putting on the baking sheet.

Recipes

Vanilla biscuits

I have used this recipe for many of the projects in the book as it makes biscuits with a smooth, flat top which are ideal for coating with icing.

INGREDIENTS

125g (4½oz) butter, at room temperature

125g (4½oz) caster sugar

1–2tsp vanilla essence

1 medium egg, lightly beaten

225g (8oz) self-raising flour

100g (3½oz) plain flour

◆ ◆ ◆ ◆ ◆

Makes approx. 18 x 7.5cm (3") biscuits

TUTOR TIPS

This recipe works best if all the ingredients are at room temperature.

I usually make this biscuit dough in a stand mixer, but you could use a hand mixer or make the dough by hand. If you are not using a stand mixer, add the flour in three parts rather than all at once.

If you would like to make coloured biscuits, add liquid food colour to the egg at step 2 before beating into the dough.

To make the dough more manageable to roll out, cut it in half and roll out two smaller sheets instead of one large one.

1 Beat the butter and sugar together in the bowl of a stand mixer until light in colour.

2 Mix the vanilla essence into the egg and gradually add to the butter and sugar, beating well between each addition.

3 Sift the flours together and tip into the bowl all at once. Mix on the slowest speed until the dough forms a ball.

4 Remove the dough from the mixer and gently knead any loose bits together.

5 Place a sheet of baking parchment on the work surface, put the dough in the centre and place another piece of parchment on top. Flatten the dough slightly with your hands.

6 Roll out the dough to a thickness of 4–5mm (¼") – use guide rings if possible to create an even thickness. Refrigerate for at least one hour.

7 Cut out the biscuits using your chosen cutter while the dough is still cold. Line a baking sheet with parchment paper then place the biscuits onto it so they are evenly spaced out. If you are making different sizes, place the smaller biscuits in the centre of the tray and the larger ones around the outside.

8 Lightly knead together the off-cuts of dough and roll out. Chill the dough again and cut out as many biscuits as you can.

9 Preheat the oven to 180°C (350°F/gas mark 4). Bake in the centre of the oven for 8–12 minutes or as per the project instructions until the biscuits are brown at the edges and are just starting to colour in the centre.

10 Leave on the baking tray for a couple of minutes then transfer to a wire rack to cool completely.

FLAVOUR VARIATIONS

Chocolate: replace 25g (just over ¾oz) of plain flour with 25g (just over ¾oz) of cocoa powder.

Orange: beat the zest of one orange with the butter before adding the sugar. Omit the vanilla if you wish.

Cinnamon: add 2tsp of ground cinnamon to the flours. Omit the vanilla if you wish.

Light gingerbread

Once baked, this recipe makes a firm biscuit particularly suited to three-dimensional and intricate designs.

INGREDIENTS

125g (4½oz) butter
115g (4oz) light muscovado sugar
50g (1¾oz) black treacle
1tsp bicarbonate of soda
275g (9¾oz) plain flour
2tsp ground ginger

Makes approx. 12 x 7.5cm (3") biscuits

TUTOR TIP

This dough does not re-roll easily, so try to cut out the biscuits as closely as possible to make the most of the dough. If you wish to re-roll, place the dough in a food-grade bag and warm in a microwave for 30 seconds to soften it slightly.

1 Melt the butter over a low heat in a small saucepan. Add the sugar and black treacle, stirring until they have dissolved. Turn off the heat.

2 Add the bicarbonate of soda and stir well. The mixture should foam slightly, becoming paler in colour.

3 Mix the flour and ginger together in a large bowl.

4 Pour the butter mixture onto the flour and stir well.

5 Place a sheet of baking parchment on the work surface and tip the dough into the centre. Place another piece of baking parchment on top and roll out to a thickness of 3–4mm (<¼") using rolling pin guides to ensure an even thickness. Allow to cool and firm up.

6 Once cool, cut out the biscuits using your chosen cutter. Line a baking sheet with parchment paper then place the biscuits onto it so they are spaced out evenly. Leave to chill for one hour.

7 Preheat the oven to 160°C (325°F/gas mark 3). Bake in the centre of the oven for 8–12 minutes or as per the project instructions, depending on the size and shape of the biscuit.

8 Leave on the baking sheet for a couple of minutes before transferring to a wire rack to cool completely.

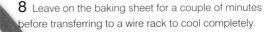

Storing biscuits

While biscuits are best eaten fresh from the oven, undecorated biscuits will keep in an airtight container for a week or more. If the biscuits have been decorated, store in a cardboard cake box to prevent them from going soft.

If you need to bake a large amount of biscuits, you can freeze the dough at different stages to make this easier. To freeze raw, cut-out biscuit dough, place the shapes on a lined baking sheet and freeze for an hour. Pack the biscuits into a freezer bag or box by layering them between sheets of baking parchment. Freeze for up to three months. Bake from frozen by adding 2–3 minutes to the baking time.

To freeze iced biscuits, place them in a single layer in an airtight freezer bag and seal well. Freeze for up to three months. Defrost in the unopened bag at room temperature. The biscuits will still be crisp but you can refresh them by putting them in an oven on a very low heat for 5–10 minutes. Add any embellishments and over-piping once defrosted.

If you don't know what shapes you will need to bake, roll out the biscuit dough between two sheets of baking parchment then place the dough on a baking sheet or cake board. Wrap well in several layers of cling film and freeze for up to three months. The sheets of dough can be stacked on top of each other. Defrost at room temperature for 30 minutes before cutting out and baking the biscuits.

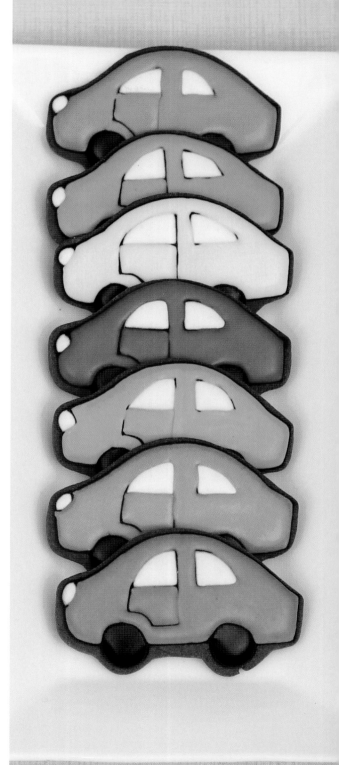

Golden Rules
for Decorating Biscuits

I have used Squires Kitchen Art-ice Cookie Icing Mix to decorate the biscuits throughout this book as it allows you to achieve the ideal consistencies for piping and run-out work easily. This instant mix has been specially formulated for decorating biscuits – it has a delicate vanilla flavour and a lovely sheen once set. Royal icing is also suitable for decorating biscuits and is available as an instant mix or can be made following your preferred recipe.

Mixing up the icing

1 Before mixing the cookie icing, check that your equipment is squeaky clean to ensure that the icing will reach the correct consistency. Sift the pack of icing mix into a bowl and beat with 75ml (2½fl oz) of cooled, boiled water until the icing forms standing peaks. It is important to beat the icing sufficiently to start with – this will take 5–10 minutes in a stand mixer using the flat beater on the slowest speed. This thick consistency is known as off-peak or piping icing (see opposite).

TUTOR TIP

Once made, always cover cookie icing with a clean, damp cloth or seal it in an airtight container. This applies to bowls of icing and any equipment you have used, such as palette knives and piping nozzles, to prevent a crust from forming.

Piping an outline

2 Fit a paper piping bag with a no. 1.5 piping nozzle (or different size as specified in the project) and fill with approximately 60g (2oz) of piping icing.

3 Pipe a continuous outline around the edge of each biscuit. When piping a straight line, hold the nozzle about 45° to the biscuit. Touch the nozzle to the biscuit, then apply a little pressure and, as soon as the icing comes out of the nozzle, lift the bag about 2.5cm (1") above the surface of the biscuit. To finish the line, reduce the pressure before you reach the end point, lower the nozzle and touch the surface before pulling away to break the icing. When piping a curved line, touch the nozzle to the biscuit, apply pressure and lift the nozzle about 2.5cm (1") above the surface at 90° to the biscuit. Finish as for the straight line.

Filling in the biscuit

4 Add 45ml (1½fl oz) of cold, pre-boiled water to the remainder of the icing to make a runnier consistency for flooding the biscuits, known as run-out icing (see opposite). Colour the icing, if required, with liquid food colour or a combination of liquid and dust colours for stronger tints.

5 Cover the bowl with a clean, damp cloth and leave for 30 minutes so that any air bubbles will rise to the top. Gently stir with a palette knife before use. If you are colouring the icing, do this before allowing the icing to stand to give the colour time to develop.

6 Half-fill a piping bag with the run-out icing and snip the tip off the bag, or use a nozzle if required. Alternatively, if you are filling in a large area you may prefer to use an icing bottle (see page 10).

7 To fill the area inside the outline with the run-out icing, hold the tip of the bag/nozzle low to the biscuit just away from the outline and apply enough pressure to force the icing to reach the outline. Continue to fill towards the centre, keeping the nozzle close to the biscuit. The icing will flow to fill small gaps but, if the gaps are large, pipe a little extra icing into them. If needed, use the tip of a slightly damp paintbrush to draw the icing right up to the piped border, particularly if there are any sharp points or corners.

8 Gently tap the biscuit on the work surface to smooth the icing and bring any remaining bubbles to the surface. Pop the bubbles with the point of a barely damp paintbrush.

9 Once you have filled the outline, leave the icing to dry. This is best done quickly under a heat source to retain a sheen on the icing and to prevent it from sinking. You can dry your iced biscuits under a desk lamp (ideal if you have lots of different sections to fill in), in a very low fan oven (50°C/120°F) or in a food dehydrator for around 20–30 minutes. (Do not leave iced biscuits in the oven for any longer than this as the fats in the biscuit can stain the icing.) Alternatively, allow the iced biscuits to air-dry at room temperature for up to 24 hours.

10 Add any final embellishments and over-piping once the biscuit is fully dry.

Storing the icing

11 Store any remaining run-out icing overnight in an airtight container at room temperature and stir again before use. It is best to use the icing within two days. Any leftover off-peak icing can be frozen for up to three months in an airtight container; defrost and re-beat before use.

Icing consistencies

Off-peak/piping icing and run-out icing are the two main consistencies you will need to use, as most of the biscuits in this book have been decorated using the outline-and-fill method described above.

Off-peak: To test whether the icing has reached off-peak consistency for piping the outline, gently press a clean palette knife onto the surface of the icing. As you pull the knife away, the icing should form a standing peak but shouldn't be too stiff. If the top of the peak flops over, beat the icing for a few minutes more. If the piping icing has been standing for some time it will become softer. For best results, beat again by hand before use.

Run-out: To test whether the icing has reached run-out consistency for filling in biscuits, draw a line through the surface of the icing with a palette knife: it should disappear after 8–10 seconds. If it takes longer, mix in a few drops of cold, pre-boiled water, stir and test again; if it disappears too quickly, add half to one teaspoon of the thicker piping icing. For best results, cover the run-out icing with a damp cloth and leave to stand for 30 minutes. Gently stir before use to burst any bubbles.

Colouring icing

Liquid food colours are best for colouring cookie icing in pastel and mid-tone colours. I use Squires Kitchen's range of liquid food colours as they don't contain glycerides/glycerol which can prevent the icing from setting.

Dust (or powder) food colours are best when you need strong, bold colours so as not to alter the consistency of the icing. After mixing through the dust colour, leave the icing to stand for at least 30 minutes to allow the colour to develop fully. You can also use a combination of liquid and dust food colours to achieve a strong colour or try mixing different coloured icings to achieve the tint you need. It's important to remember that the icing will dry a shade or so darker than when it is wet.

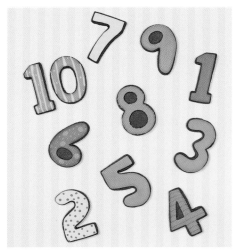

Black is a very hard colour to mix up, so where a large quantity is needed I have used Squires Kitchen's ready-coloured Instant Mix Royal Icing in Tuxedo Black. For smaller quantities you can colour the icing with black dust food colour, but be aware that a considerable amount is needed to reach a true black.

TIPS FOR COLOURING ICING

If you need to make up several batches of icing that are the same colour, weigh the icing and count the drops of liquid colour you use to achieve that exact shade again.

If you are using the same colour to pipe the outline and fill the biscuit, colour the icing at off-peak stage to pipe the outline then let the remaining icing down to run-out consistency so that it is exactly the same colour.

If you are using several different colours of run-out icing, colour the icing once it has been thinned down.

Tips and Tricks for Icing Biscuits

You will find step-by-step instructions with each project, but there are a few tips and tricks that will help you achieve perfectly iced biscuits every time. Once you have mastered the basics you can create your own biscuit designs using your piping skills.

☆ Prepare all the icing for each stage of the project by making it to the required consistency, colouring it then transferring it into piping bags or bottles before starting to decorate. Cover any icing to be used later with a clean, damp cloth or seal it in an airtight container.

☆ Always use the thicker, off-peak icing to pipe around the outer edge and to outline the shapes within a biscuit, piping from the centre to the outside.

☆ The outline can either be disguised or used as a design feature as shown here. To pipe an outline as a contrast to the fill colour, use a no. 2 or 3 nozzle to pipe the outline to ensure it stands out from the fill colour.

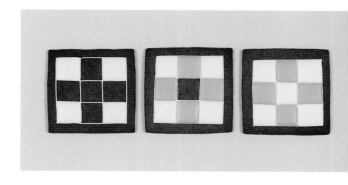

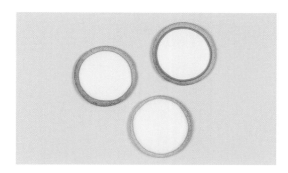

☆ To achieve an invisible outline, use the same colour icing for the outline and fill and use a no. 1 or 1.5 nozzle. This is only practical where one colour is being used; making up a series of matching outline and fill icings is very time consuming. Where a number of different fill colours are in contact with the outline you can disguise the outline by colouring it to match the colour of the biscuit.

☆ Where designs have adjacent areas to be filled (either with the same or different colours) they must not be filled at the same time as the icing will blend together. Allow the icing in one area to dry slightly, to the point where it has lost its shine, before filling an area next to it. This usually takes about 10 minutes but can be sped up by placing the biscuit under a desk lamp.

☆ Where a small quantity of cookie icing is needed, weigh out the amount you require and adjust the water accordingly before preparing in the usual way. Keep the rest of the packet sealed in an airtight container until needed and sieve the contents into a bowl before use.

☆ If cookie icing is left to stand for several hours, either in a piping bottle/bag or bowl, the icing will separate into a dark lower layer and pale top layer. Always stir it back to a consistent colour to ensure a streak-free finish and, if necessary, empty piping bags/bottles back into the bowl, stir and refill.

☆ You can practise the outline-and-fill technique without baking by using a packet of plain, shop-bought biscuits.

Numbers

Anniversary Biscuits

EDIBLES

Vanilla biscuit dough (see recipe on pages 12–13)

500g (1lb 1¾oz) SK Art-Ice Cookie Icing Mix

25: SK Black Quality Food Colour (QFC) Liquid, SK Silver Designer Metallic Lustre Dust Food Colour

30: SK White Satin Designer Bridal Satin Lustre Dust Food Colour

40: SK Poinsettia Professional Liquid Food Colour, SK Black Quality Food Colour (QFC) Liquid, SK Ruby Designer Moon Beam Dust Food Colour

50: SK Professional Liquid Food Colours: Chestnut and Sunflower, SK Classic Gold Designer Metallic Lustre Dust Food Colour

60: SK Ice White Designer Fairy Sparkles Dust Food Colour, Crystal White Magic Sparkles Edible Glitter Sprinkles

EQUIPMENT

Essential equipment (see pages 8–9)

Number cutter set

Piping nozzles: nos. 1.5, 2

Small piece of food-grade sponge

SK Paintbrush: no. 10 (flat)

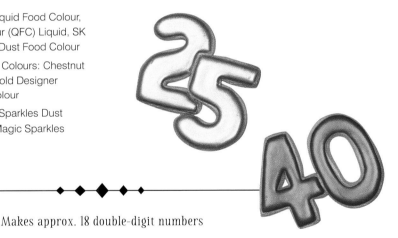

Makes approx. 18 double-digit numbers

Cutting out the biscuits

1 Prepare and roll out the vanilla biscuit dough following the recipe on pages 12–13. Cut out your chosen anniversary numerals from the dough.

2 Place the first numeral onto a lined baking sheet, then cut away a small section of the biscuit in order to fit the second numeral against it with the second numeral cutter. Place the second numeral into the cut-away shape so that the biscuits fit together neatly. Repeat with all the biscuits. Do not move the biscuits once you've stuck them together.

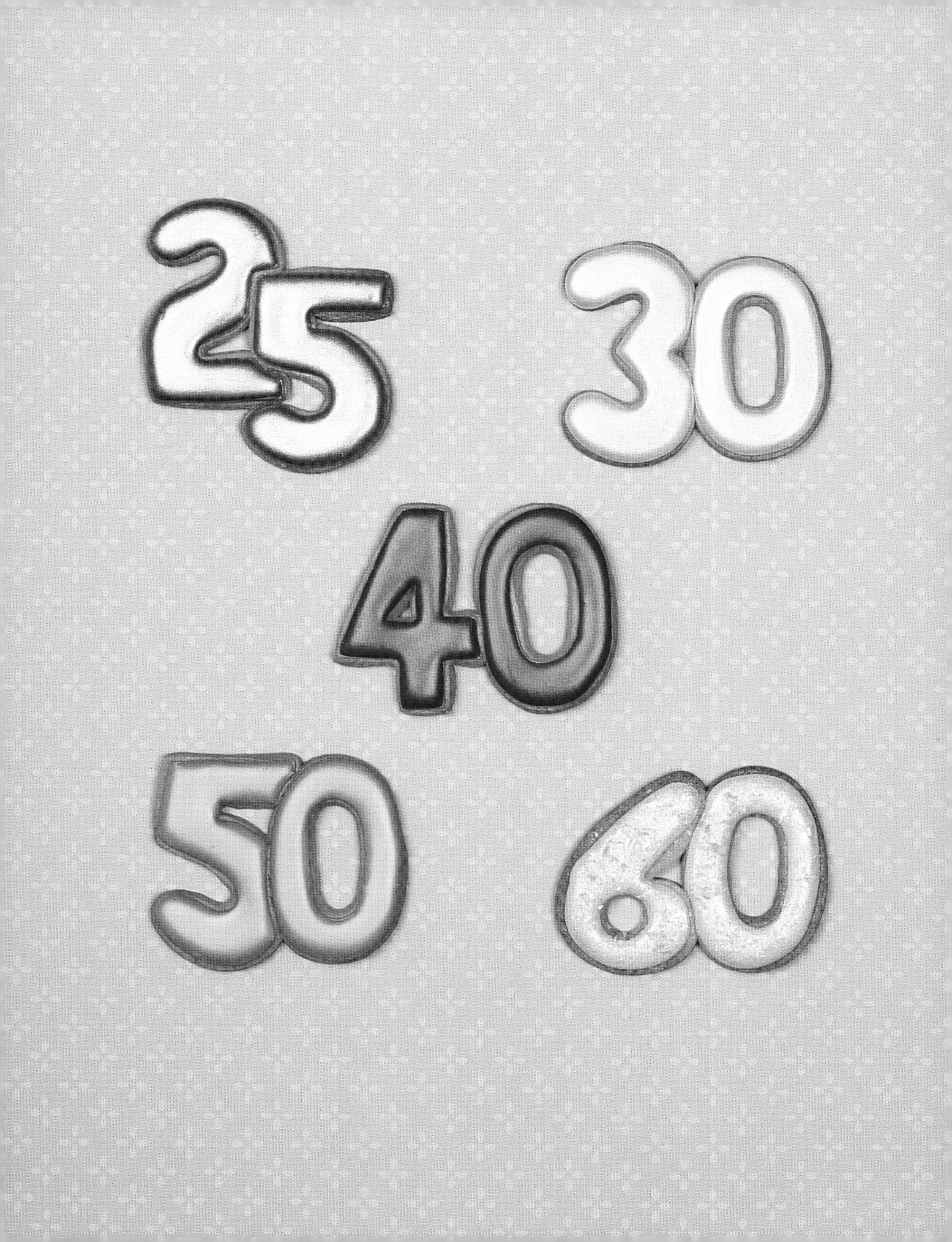
25
30
40
50
60

3 Bake the biscuits for 8–10 minutes following the recipe.

Making and colouring the icing

4 Beat all the cookie icing mix with 75ml (2½oz) of cooled, boiled water until it forms standing peaks (see page 17). Leave the icing uncoloured if you are making the 30th or 60th anniversary biscuits. For the other biscuits, colour the icing as follows:

25th anniversary: add a little Black liquid food colour to make grey.

40th anniversary: add a generous amount of Poinsettia and a little touch of Black liquid food colours to make ruby red.

50th anniversary: add Chestnut and Sunflower liquid food colours to make gold.

5 Weigh out 60g (2oz) of piping icing into a separate bowl. Add 45ml (1½oz) of cooled, boiled water to the remainder of the icing to make run-out icing (see page 17).

6 Fit a small piping bag with a no. 1.5 nozzle and half-fill with the thick piping icing. Fill an icing bottle with the thin run-out icing and attach a no. 2 nozzle.

Decorating the biscuits

7 Use the piping icing to outline each number then fill the first number of each biscuit with the run-out icing.

8 Set your oven to a low temperature (50°C/120°F) and place the biscuits in the oven to dry for 5–10 minutes (or dry under a lamp if you prefer).

9 Remove the biscuits from the oven, allow to cool for a couple of minutes then fill in the second number of each one with run-out icing.

10 Return all of the iced biscuits to the oven for 30 minutes, then leave to air-dry for at least 12 hours until completely dry.

11 Use a small piece of food-grade sponge to smear a little white vegetable fat over each of the biscuits. Wipe off any excess fat with a piece of

kitchen paper.

12 To finish, carefully brush each biscuit with lustre dust food colour as follows:

25th anniversary: Silver.

30th anniversary: White Satin.

40th anniversary: Ruby.

50th anniversary: Classic Gold.

60th anniversary: brush with Ice White dust, then dab with a little edible glue and sprinkle with Crystal White Magic Sparkles.

TUTOR TIP

When using dust food colours, always try to build up the lustre dust gradually. Tip a small amount onto a piece of kitchen paper, dip the paintbrush into it and tap off any excess before brushing onto the biscuit.

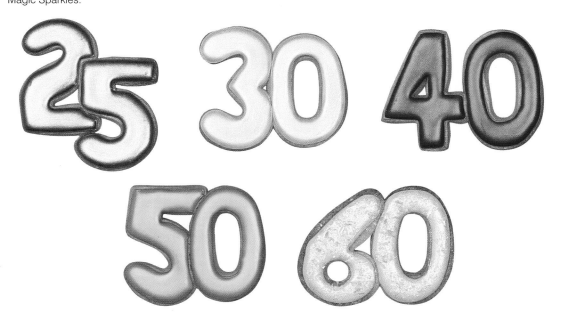

Birthday Numerals

EDIBLES

Chocolate biscuit dough (see recipe on pages 12–13)

500g (1lb 1¾oz) SK Art-Ice Cookie Icing Mix

SK Professional Liquid Food Colours: Bulrush, Daffodil, Hyacinth, Poinsettia

EQUIPMENT

Essential equipment (see pages 8–9)

Number cutter set

Piping nozzle: no. 1.5

5 small icing bottles with no. 2 nozzles

Makes approx. 36 biscuits

Cutting out the biscuits

1 Prepare and roll out the chocolate biscuit dough following the recipe on pages 12–13. Cut out the biscuits using the number cutters while the dough is cold.

2 Line a baking sheet with parchment paper then place the biscuits onto it so they are evenly spaced out. Bake the biscuits for 8–9 minutes.

TUTOR TIP

Depending on the cutters you are using, you may wish to leave the central part of the numbers rather than cutting them out as this will give you more biscuit.

Making and colouring the icing

3 Beat all the cookie icing mix with 75ml (2½oz) of cooled, boiled water until it forms standing peaks (see page 17). Weigh out 60g (2oz) of the thick piping icing into a separate bowl and colour with Bulrush liquid food colour until it is just lighter than the colour of the biscuits. Cut off the end of a piping bag, drop a no. 1.5 nozzle into the bottom and half-fill with the brown piping icing.

4 Add 45ml (1½oz) of cooled, boiled water to the remainder of the icing to make run-out icing (see page 17). Divide the run-out icing between three bowls, one containing more icing than the other two. Colour the larger amount of icing with Daffodil liquid food colour and each of the smaller quantities with Hyacinth and Poinsettia.

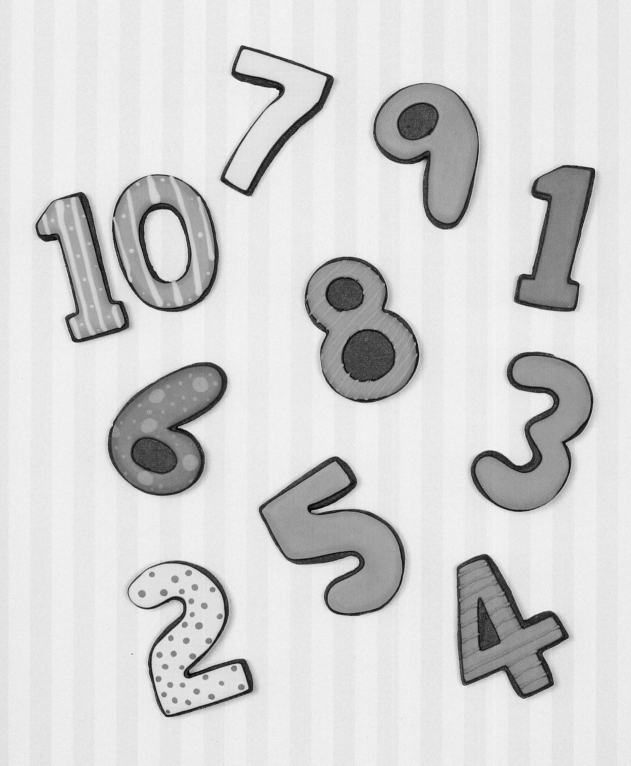

5 In another bowl, mix 1tbsp of the Daffodil-coloured icing with the same amount of Hyacinth-coloured icing to make green. Add a little more yellow or blue to adjust the colour if required.

6 In a fifth bowl, mix 1tbsp of the Daffodil-coloured icing with the same amount of Poinsettia-coloured icing to make orange.

7 Half-fill five small piping bags with the coloured run-out icings (no nozzle required).

8 Carefully pour the remaining icing into five piping bottles and fit each bottle with a no. 2 nozzle.

Decorating the biscuits

9 Use the brown piping icing to outline each of the biscuits, not forgetting to outline the centres of the 4, 6, 8, 9 and 0.

10 To coat a biscuit, take one of the icing bottles and pipe the icing against the outline and then fill them in. If the icing is uneven or goes over the outline, use a damp paintbrush to smooth it out. At this point you have the option to leave the biscuit plain or add a pattern.

11 To pattern the biscuits with dots and stripes cut a very small hole at the end of each of the filled piping bags when you're ready to use it and check that the icing comes out smoothly. If not, cut the hole slightly bigger.

12 To make dots, coat a single biscuit as described in step 10 then immediately drop small blobs of run-out icing into the wet icing, either keeping the blobs the same size or varying their size. Gently tap the biscuit to settle the icing.

13 For stripes, coat a single biscuit as described in step 10 then immediately pipe a thin line of coloured run-out icing across the biscuit. Very light pressure will result in a thin line while firmer pressure will leave a thicker line. Gently tap the biscuit to settle the icing.

14 Repeat the same method to make a range of colourful designs on all the biscuits. Arrange them on a baking sheet and place them in an oven on a low temperature (50°C/120°F) to dry for 5–10 minutes.

TUTOR TIP

When using icing bottles keep them upside down in a straight-sided container lined at the bottom with clean, damp kitchen paper. This will prevent the nozzle drying up so the icing is always ready to be piped.

Milestone Birthdays

EDIBLES

Vanilla biscuit dough (see recipe on pages 12–13)

500g (1lb 1¾oz) SK Art-Ice Cookie Icing Mix

Rose design:

SK Professional Liquid Food Colours: Chestnut, Leaf Green, Poinsettia, Rose

Tartan design:

SK Professional Liquid Food Colours: Bluebell, Fern, Leaf Green, Poinsettia, Sunflower

EQUIPMENT

Essential equipment (see pages 8–9)

Number cutter set

Piping nozzle: no. 1.5

Piping bottle/plastic piping bag with no. 2 nozzle or medium paper piping bag with no nozzle

Colour mixing palette

Makes approx. 18 double-digit numbers

Cutting out the biscuits

1 Prepare and roll out the vanilla biscuit dough following the recipe on pages 12–13. Cut out your chosen double-digit numerals from the dough.

2 Place the first number onto a lined baking sheet, decide how the second number will be attached and use the cutter to cut away the dough from the first number.

Cut out and place the second number into the cut-away shape, making sure the numerals fit together neatly with several points of contact. Do not move the biscuits once they are stuck together.

3 Repeat to make approximately 18 double-digit numbers then bake for 8–10 minutes following the recipe.

Making and colouring the icing

4 Beat all the cookie icing mix with 75ml (2½oz) of cooled, boiled water until it forms standing peaks (see page 17). Weigh out 60g (2oz) of piping icing into a separate bowl and colour this with Chestnut liquid colour so that it is a similar light brown colour to the biscuits. Add 45ml (1½oz) of cooled, boiled water to the remainder of the icing to make run-out icing (see page 17). You can then choose to ice the biscuits in either the rose or tartan pattern.

Rose design

5 Fit a small paper piping bag with a no. 1.5 nozzle and half-fill with the light brown piping icing.

6 Place a tablespoon of the thin run-out icing into each of three bowls and colour as follows: one with Leaf Green, one with Rose to make a mid-pink and one with Poinsettia to make a dark pink. Half-fill small piping bags without nozzles with the three colours.

7 Leave the remainder of the run-out icing white and fill an icing bottle fitted with a no. 2 nozzle.

8 Outline the numbers with the bag of light brown piping icing.

9 Cut a very small hole at the end of each small piping bag and check that the icing comes out smoothly. If not, cut the hole slightly bigger.

10 Pour a little Leaf Green liquid colour into one of the wells of the mixing palette. Have a damp cloth to hand.

11 Fill the first digit with the white run-out icing and immediately create the rose pattern. Drop dots of varying sizes in mid-pink icing into the background colour, followed by a small comma shape of deep pink. Swirl the two pinks together with a scribing tool in a random pattern, spreading the dark pink into the light pink to look like a rose.

12 When you have finished all the roses, pipe a dot of green icing next to each one. Dip the tip of the scribing tool into the liquid colour in the palette, place into the centre of the green dot and pull the point out in a curve to create a leaf shape. Clean the scribing tool on a damp cloth before moving onto the next leaf.

TUTOR TIP

If there is too much green colour on the scribing tool, dab it lightly onto kitchen paper to remove the excess.

13 Set aside to dry for 5–10 minutes then pipe the second numeral in the same way. Allow the biscuit to dry completely.

Tartan design

14 Fit a small piping bag with a no. 1.5 piping nozzle and half-fill with the light brown piping icing.

15 Place a tablespoon of the thin run-out icing into each of three bowls and colour as follows: one with Poinsettia, one with Bluebell and one with Sunflower. Half-fill three small piping bags with no nozzles.

16 Colour the remainder of the run-out icing Fern and fill an icing bottle/large piping bag fitted with a no. 2 nozzle.

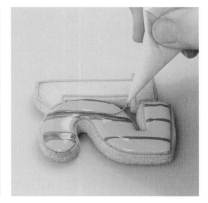

20 Turn the biscuit 90° and repeat step 19 to make a check pattern.

21 Pipe yellow lines between the red/blue ones in one direction, then turn the biscuit 90° and repeat to complete the pattern.

22 Repeat the same method on the first digit of each biscuit then set aside to dry for 5–10 minutes before filling in and decorating the second digit. Allow to dry completely.

TUTOR TIP

Before decorating the biscuits, practise making the patterns by piping some run-out icing onto a clean plate and creating the rose and/or tartan patterns.

17 Outline the numbers with the light brown piping icing.

18 Cut a very small hole in the end of each bag of coloured run-out icing and check the icing flows out smoothly. Fill the first digit with green run-out icing then add the pattern immediately following the steps below while the icing is still wet.

19 Pipe equally spaced, vertical red lines onto the number. Pipe a dark blue line on either side of each red line.

TUTOR TIP

You can design your own tartan pattern on squared paper before decorating your biscuits. Check the pattern will fit by holding the biscuit over your design.

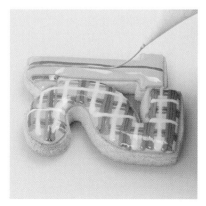  

Letters

BABY

A New Arrival

EDIBLES

Vanilla biscuit dough (see pages 12–13)

500g (1lb 1¾oz) SK Art-Ice Cookie Icing Mix

SK Professional Liquid Food Colours: Lilac, Mint

EQUIPMENT

Essential equipment (see pages 8–9)

Letter cutters (approx. 5cm/2" high)

Piping nozzles: 3 x no. 2

Makes approx. 10 biscuits

Cutting out the biscuits

1 Prepare and roll out the vanilla biscuit dough following the recipe on pages 12–13. Cut out enough letters to make approximately ten 'BABY' biscuits.

2 Place the first 'B' on a lined baking tray and use the cutter for the 'A' to remove the dough where the letters will overlap. Position the 'A' neatly against the first 'B'. Repeat this for the other letters to spell out 'BABY'. Do not move the biscuit once the word is complete.

3 Repeat step 2 to make all the remaining biscuits.

4 Bake for approximately 10–12 minutes following the recipe.

TUTOR TIP

To ensure the letters are level on the tray, draw a line on the baking parchment with a food colour pen and place this side down on the tray. Place the base of each letter on the line.

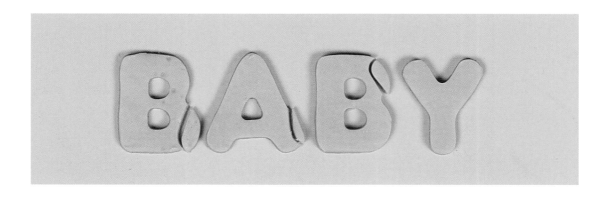

Making and the colouring the icing

5 Beat all the cookie icing mix with 75ml (2½oz) of cooled, boiled water until it forms standing peaks (see page 17). Weigh out 60g (2oz) of piping icing into a separate bowl. Add 45ml (1½oz) of cooled, boiled water to the remainder of the icing to make run-out icing (see page 17).

6 Divide the thick piping icing between three bowls. Leave one bowl white, colour one with a little Mint liquid food colour and one with a little Lilac liquid food colour to make pastel tones. Fit three small piping bags with no. 2 nozzles and half-fill with each colour.

7 Divide the run-out icing between three bowls. Leave one white, colour one pale Mint and the third pale Lilac. Half-fill three medium paper piping bags with the three colours.

Decorating the biscuits

8 Before you start piping, decide on your colour scheme to avoid two adjacent letters being outlined and/or filled with the same colours.

9 Outline each letter in a different coloured piping icing.

10 Fill every other letter with contrasting coloured run-out icing and set aside to dry under a lamp for 5–10 minutes.

11 Fill the remaining letters with different coloured run-out icings. Set aside to dry completely.

Love Me Do

EDIBLES

Vanilla biscuit dough (see pages 12–13)

500g (1lb 1¾oz) SK Art-Ice Cookie Icing Mix

SK Professional Liquid Food Colour: Rose

EQUIPMENT

Essential equipment (see pages 8–9)

Letter cutters (approx. 5cm/2" high)

Piping nozzles: 2 x no. 2

◆ ◆ ◆ ◆ ◆

Makes approx. 10 biscuits

Cutting out the biscuits

1 Prepare and roll out the vanilla biscuit dough following the recipe on pages 12–13. Cut out enough letters to make approximately ten 'LOVE' biscuits.

2 Place a letter 'L' on a lined baking tray and use the cutter for the 'O' to remove the dough where the letters will overlap. Position the 'O' against the 'L'. Repeat until you have spelt out 'LOVE'. Do not move the biscuit once the word is complete.

3 Repeat step 2 to make all the remaining biscuits.

4 Bake for approximately 10–12 minutes following the recipe.

Making and colouring the icing

5 Beat all the cookie icing mix with 75ml (2½oz) of cooled, boiled water until it forms standing peaks (see page 17). Weigh out 60g (2oz) of piping icing into a separate bowl. Add 45ml (1½oz) of cooled, boiled water to the remainder of the icing to make run-out icing (see page 17).

6 Divide the thick piping icing between two bowls.

Colour one with Rose liquid food colour and leave one white. Fit two small piping bags with no. 2 nozzles and half-fill with icing.

7 Divide the run-out icing equally between two bowls. Colour one half the same shade of Rose as the piping icing and leave the other half white. Fill two icing bottles with the run-out icing and fit them with no. 2 nozzles.

Decorating the biscuits

8 Outline the letters in alternating colours of piping icing.

9 Fill the first letter with run-out icing in the same colour as the outline. Immediately drop dots of the contrasting run-out icing along the centre of the letter. Place the tip of a scribing tool into the wet icing just above the dot at the top and gently pull the tip down through all of the dots in one motion to create a row of hearts. Clean the scribing tool.

10 Repeat step 9 on the letter 'V'. Set aside to dry for 5–10 minutes.

11 Repeat step 9 on the 'O' and 'E' in reverse colours. Set aside to dry fully.

Party Balloons

EDIBLES

Vanilla biscuit dough (see pages 12–13)
500g (1lb 1¾oz) SK Art-Ice Cookie Icing Mix
SK Professional Food Colours: Chestnut, Gentian

EQUIPMENT

Essential equipment (see pages 8–9)
SK Round Balloon Cookie Cutter
Piping nozzles: nos. 1.5, 2

Makes 12 biscuits

Cutting out the biscuits

1 Prepare and roll out the vanilla biscuit dough following the recipe on pages 12–13. Cut out 12 biscuits using the balloon cutter then bake for approximately 10–12 minutes.

Making and the colouring the icing

2 Beat all the cookie icing mix with 75ml (2½fl oz) of cooled, boiled water until it forms standing peaks (see page 17). Weigh out 60g (2oz) of piping icing into a separate bowl and colour this with Chestnut liquid food colour to make a light brown, similar to the biscuits.

3 Add 45ml (1½fl oz) of cooled, boiled water to the remainder of the icing to make run-out icing (see page 17). Transfer 2tbsp of white run-out icing into a separate bowl and put this aside. Add one or two drops of Gentian liquid food colour to the remaining run-out icing to make a light blue colour.

4 Fit a small piping bag with a no. 2 nozzle and half-fill with the light brown piping icing.

5 Fit a small piping bag with a no. 1.5 nozzle and half-fill with the white run-out icing.

6 Fill a piping bottle with the blue run-out icing and attach a no. 2 nozzle.

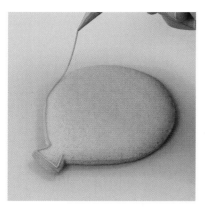 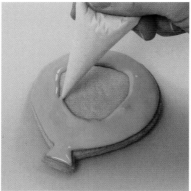 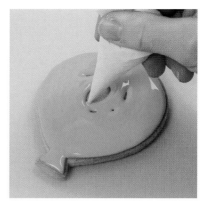

Decorating the biscuits

7 Outline each of the balloon biscuits with light brown piping icing.

8 Fill in the outline of the first balloon biscuit with light blue run-out icing, starting around the edge of the balloon shape and working towards the centre.

9 Immediately use the white icing to pipe two thin shine lines at the edge of the biscuit, tapering them to a thin point. If necessary, gently pull a scribing tool through the white icing to help shape the shine lines.

10 Use the same bag of white icing to write your chosen name across the middle of the balloon on some or all of the biscuits. Set aside to dry fully.

11 Repeat steps 8–10 to decorate half of the biscuits.

TUTOR TIP

Spread a little run-out icing onto a clean plate then practise piping your chosen name in a contrasting colour.

12 For the dark blue biscuits, empty any leftover blue icing back into the bowl and add a few more drops of Gentian to make a deeper shade. Fill a clean bottle with the icing, attach a no. 2 nozzle and repeat steps 8–10 to decorate the remaining biscuits.

Planes, Trains
and Automobiles

Road Trip

EDIBLES

Chocolate biscuit dough (see recipe on pages 12–13)

500g (1lb 1¾oz) SK Art-Ice Cookie Icing Mix

100g (3½oz) SK Tuxedo Black Professional Instant Mix Royal Icing

SK Professional Liquid Food Colours: Berberis, Bulrush, Daffodil, Fuchsia, Hyacinth, Hydrangea, Mint, Poinsettia

SK Black Food Colour Pen

EQUIPMENT

Essential equipment (see pages 8–9)

Small car cutter

SK Black Food Colour Pen

9 small bowls

Piping nozzle: no. 1.5

Makes approx. 28 biscuits

Cutting out the biscuits

1 Prepare and roll out the chocolate biscuit dough following the recipe on pages 12–13. Cut out as many biscuits as you can using the car cutter, then bake the biscuits for 7–8 minutes.

Making and colouring the icing

2 Beat all the cookie icing mix with 75ml (2½oz) of cooled, boiled water until it forms standing peaks (see page 17). Weigh out 60g (2oz) of piping icing into a separate bowl. Add 45ml (1½oz) of cooled, boiled water to the remainder of the icing to make run-out icing (see page 17).

3 Colour the piping icing with Bulrush liquid food colour to make a similar colour to the biscuits.

4 Divide the run-out icing between seven small bowls, leaving a small amount white. Colour the other bowls

of icing with Berberis, Daffodil, Fuchsia, Hyacinth, Hydrangea, Mint and Poinsettia liquid food colours respectively.

5 To make up the black icing, shake the bag well and measure out 100g (3½oz) of royal icing powder into a clean bowl. Add 15ml (3tsp) of cooled, boiled water and stir vigorously for 5–10 minutes until the icing is thick. Gently stir in a further 1–2tsp of water until the black icing is a similar consistency to the coloured run-out icing.

TUTOR TIP

If you do not want to make the black icing by hand then make a slightly larger quantity using a stand mixer. Weigh out no less than 200g (7oz) of royal icing powder and add the appropriate amount of water (30ml for 200g). Any remaining icing can be frozen for use another time.

Decorating the biscuits

6 Use the black food colour pen to draw the wheels, door, windows, headlights and chassis outline on the biscuits.

7 Fit a small piping bag with a no. 1.5 nozzle and half-fill with brown piping icing. Pipe over the details on each car.

8 Half-fill a medium piping bag with white run-out icing, snip off the tip of the bag and fill in the windows and headlights.

9 Half-fill a medium piping bag with black run-out icing, snip off the tip of the bag and fill in the wheels. Set the biscuits aside to dry for 5–10 minutes.

10 Half-fill seven medium piping bags with each colour of run-out icing and snip off the tip of the bags. Fill in just the door of 3–5 cars with the first colour. Set aside to dry.

11 Repeat with the next colour and continue until all the doors are filled in.

12 Fill in the body of each car in the same order and colour as the doors. Set aside to dry completely.

TUTOR TIP

Once you've snipped off the tip of the bag, check the icing comes out smoothly. If not, you may need to cut a slightly larger hole.

TUTOR TIP

If your run-out icing looks streaky once it has been piped, it has started to separate in the piping bag. Squeeze the icing back into the bowl, stir gently and fill a new piping bag.

Toy Train

EDIBLES

Vanilla biscuit dough (see recipe on pages 12–13)

500g (1lb 1¾oz) SK Art-Ice Cookie Icing Mix

100g (3½oz) SK Tuxedo Black Professional Instant Mix Royal Icing

SK Professional Liquid Food Colours: Chestnut, Fern, Hyacinth, Poppy

EQUIPMENT

Essential equipment (see pages 8–9)

Square cutters: 45mm, 80mm, 95mm (1¾", 3⅛", 3¾")

Round cutters: 25mm, 30mm 40mm (1", 1⅛", 1½")

Piping nozzles: 2 x no. 2

Makes approx. one engine, one tender (coal car) and six carriage biscuits

Cutting out the biscuits

1 For the steam engine, cut out one 95mm (3¾") square biscuit and place it onto a lined baking tray. Use the 45mm (1¾") square cutter to remove the top left corner. Cut a small rectangle from the cut-out piece to use as the funnel.

2 At the base of the engine, cut out semicircles for the wheel arches using the 30mm and 40mm (1⅛" and 1½") round cutters. Use the 25mm (1") round cutter to make a window in the engine.

3 For the tender (coal car), cut out one 80mm (3⅛") square biscuit and place it onto the lined baking tray. Cut it in half, then slice off a slim piece from the top to use as the roof of the steam engine. Cut the top of the remaining piece into a cloud shape. Use the 30mm (1⅛") round cutter to cut out the wheel arches.

4 For the carriages, cut out six 80mm (3⅛") square biscuits and place them onto a lined baking tray. Cut out the wheel arches as before.

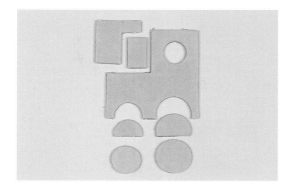

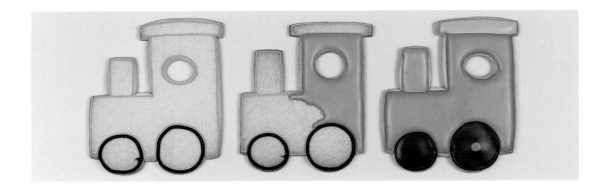

5 Use the 25mm (1") round cutter to cut out two wheels for each carriage, two for the tender and one for the engine. Cut one 40mm (1½") wheel for the engine. Fit the wheels into the wheel arches on all the biscuits.

6 Bake the biscuits for 10–12 minutes following the recipe on pages 12–13.

TUTOR TIP

To help the biscuits maintain their shape, make sure the dough is well chilled before the pieces are cut out and move the pieces as little as possible. Fit the biscuits together on a baking sheet and leave lots of space around each biscuit.

Making and colouring the icing

7 Beat all the cookie icing mix with 75ml (2½oz) of cooled, boiled water until it forms standing peaks (see page 17). Weigh out 60g (2oz) of piping icing into a separate bowl. Add 45ml (1½oz) of cooled, boiled water to the remaining icing to make a thin, run-out consistency (see page 17).

8 Colour the thick piping icing with Chestnut liquid food colour to make a pale biscuit colour. Fit a small piping bag with a no. 2 nozzle and half-fill with the icing.

9 Half-fill a small paper piping bag with white run-out icing and reserve a tablespoon of the icing in a small bowl.

10 Divide the rest of the run-out icing between three bowls and colour with Fern, Hyacinth and Poppy liquid food colours respectively. Half-fill three piping bags with the coloured icing and snip a small hole in the tip.

11 To make up the black icing, shake the bag of royal icing well and measure out 100g (3½oz) of powder into a clean bowl. Add 15ml (3tsp) of cooled, boiled water and stir vigorously for 5–10 minutes until the icing is thick. Fit a small piping bag with a no. 2 nozzle and half-fill with icing.

Decorating the biscuits

12 Use the bag of Chestnut-coloured icing to pipe an outline around the engine, tender and carriages, including the windows and door. Use the black icing to outline the wheels.

TUTOR TIP

If you aren't confident at piping the details straight onto the biscuits you can draw outlines on the biscuits with an edible food pen as a guideline (see page 49).

13 Fill in the main section of the steam engine with the red run-out icing and set aside to dry.

14 Fill in the main sections of the tender and carriage biscuits with the green or blue run-out icing. Set aside to dry.

15 Fill in the roof of the engine biscuit with the green run-out icing and the funnel with the blue run-out icing.

16 Pipe the coal on the tender biscuit with thick, black piping icing. Hold the nozzle close to the biscuit and use firm pressure to pipe mounds of black icing.

17 Fill in the windows of the train carriages with white run-out icing. Leave to dry for 5–10 minutes then fill in the door with blue run-out icing. Set aside to dry.

18 Squeeze any remaining thick, black icing into a bowl and add a few drops of cooled, boiled water. Stir gently until the consistency is similar to the coloured run-out icing.

19 Half-fill a medium piping bag and fill the wheels on the first biscuit with the black run-out icing. Immediately pipe a drop of the corresponding coloured run-out icing into the centre of the wheel. Repeat for all the remaining biscuits.

Aeroplane Biscuits

EDIBLES

Vanilla biscuit dough (see recipe on pages 12–13)

500g (1lb 1¾oz) SK Art-Ice Cookie Icing Mix

SK Professional Liquid Food Colours: Gentian, Hyacinth, Mint and Poinsettia

SK Orange Food Colour Pen

EQUIPMENT

Essential equipment (see pages 8–9)

Aeroplane cookie cutter

Ruler

Pizza cutter (optional)

Piping nozzles: 2 x no. 1.5

Piping bottle with no. 1.5 nozzle

Makes approx. 12 3-D biscuits

Cutting out the biscuits

1 Prepare and roll out the vanilla biscuit dough following the recipe on pages 12–13. Measure the width of the fuselage and wingspan of the cutter and cut strips of biscuit dough slightly wider than each using a pizza wheel or sharp knife. Cut out an equal number of wings, fuselages and tail pieces and place them on a lined baking sheet as you go.

2 Use a small, sharp knife to trim the top of the fuselage to a curved shape and the base flat.

3 Trim the wings so they are just under 2.5cm (1") wide across the central area.

4 Cut a notch in the tail piece of the body measuring 5mm (¹⁄₈") long and 5mm (¹⁄₈") wide and a corresponding one in the cut-out tail pieces.

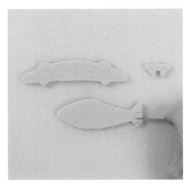

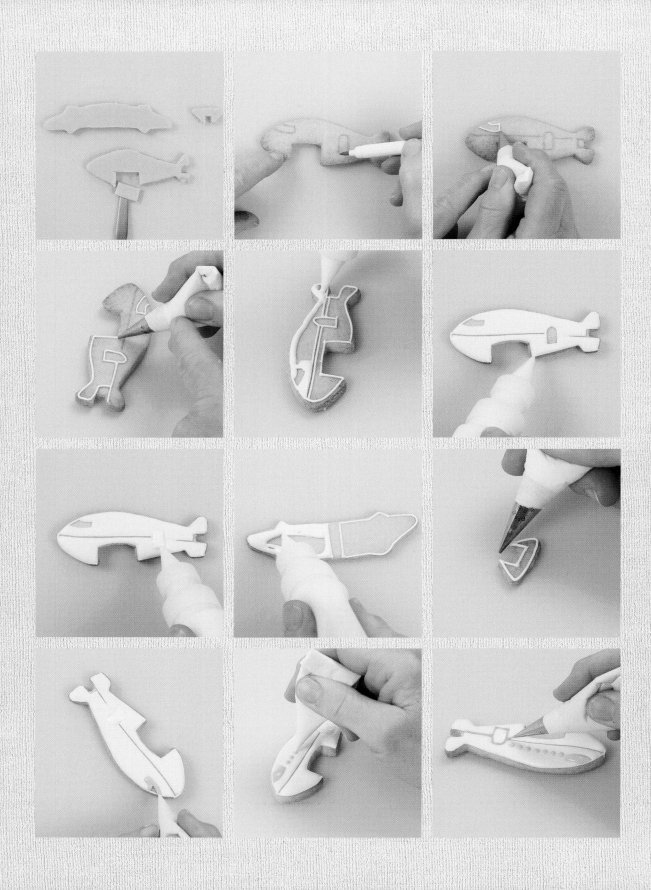

5 Using the picture as a guide, cut out a small oblong measuring 2.5cm x 1cm (1" x $^3/_8$") from the base of the plane.

6 Bake all the biscuit pieces for approximately 8–10 minutes following the recipe.

TUTOR TIP

Place the small tail pieces in the centre of the baking sheet and the larger biscuits around the edges so that they bake evenly.

Making and colouring the icing

7 Beat all the cookie icing mix with 75ml (2½oz) of cooled, boiled water until it forms standing peaks (see page 17). Weigh out 60g (2oz) of piping icing into a separate bowl. Add 45ml (1½oz) of cooled, boiled water to the remainder of the icing to make run-out icing (see page 17).

8 Keep 30g (1oz) of the thicker piping icing white and divide the remainder into three separate bowls. Colour with Hyacinth, Mint and Poinsettia liquid food colours. Fit a small piping bag with a no. 1.5 nozzle and half-fill with white piping icing. Keep the bowls of coloured icing and the remaining white icing covered to use later.

9 Place a generous tablespoon of the thin run-out icing into a bowl and colour with a little Gentian liquid colour to make a pale blue. Half-fill a small piping bag with no nozzle.

10 Pour the white run-out icing into an icing bottle or piping bag with a no. 1.5 nozzle.

Decorating the biscuits

11 The notches cut in the raw dough may expand or become misshapen during cooking so check the fit of the fuselage, wings and tail pieces. If necessary, carefully scrape the notches to shape using a sharp knife.

12 Use the edible food colour pen to draw guidelines onto the biscuits, following the pictures as a guide.

13 Use the bag of white piping icing with the no. 1.5 nozzle to pipe outlines on all the pieces. Outline the door first, the double line down the side of the plane, the cockpit window and then around the outside of the plane, wing and tail piece. Leave a gap on either side of the oblong cut out of the fuselage, down the centre of the wings and at the narrow edge of the notches in the tail pieces so that the biscuits will slot together.

14 Use the white run-out icing to fill in the main body of the plane, wings and tail pieces. Do not fill the windows or door yet. Set aside to dry for 10 minutes or so.

15 Cut a very small hole in the piping bag with the pale blue run-out icing and fill in the cockpit window. Drop in a very small dot of white run-out icing and use a scriber to drag this into a teardrop shape.

16 Pipe small dots of the pale blue icing across the top half of the fuselage to represent the cabin windows. Fill the door with white run-out icing then set aside to dry for 10 minutes or so.

17 Fit a small piping bag with a no. 1.5 nozzle and half-fill with one of the thick, coloured piping icings. Outline the door and then drop a line between the upper and lower parts of the fuselage on four of the planes. Clean the nozzle, fill a new bag with a second colour and repeat, then do the same with the third colour. Allow biscuits to dry fully.

Constructing the 3D planes

18 Place the remaining white piping icing in a small piping bag and cut a small hole in the tip.

19 Fit the tail piece by piping icing into the notch on the plane and pushing the additional piece into place. Clear away any icing which squeezes out with a slightly damp paintbrush. Set aside to dry for a few minutes.

20 Pipe a generous line of icing along the notch in the centre of the fuselage and push the wings into place. Hold until firm then neaten with a paintbrush, as before.

21 Pipe a little extra icing around the joins and use a paintbrush to neaten them up. Allow to dry completely.

TUTOR TIP

If the biscuits will be seen from both sides, repeat steps 12–17 on the reverse of each fuselage biscuit, ensuring that the icing on the first side is completely dry before you start. Decorate the back of the biscuit first.

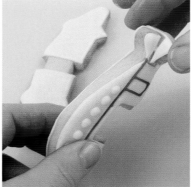
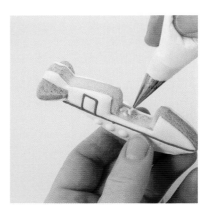

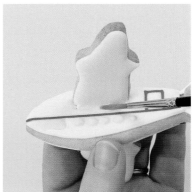

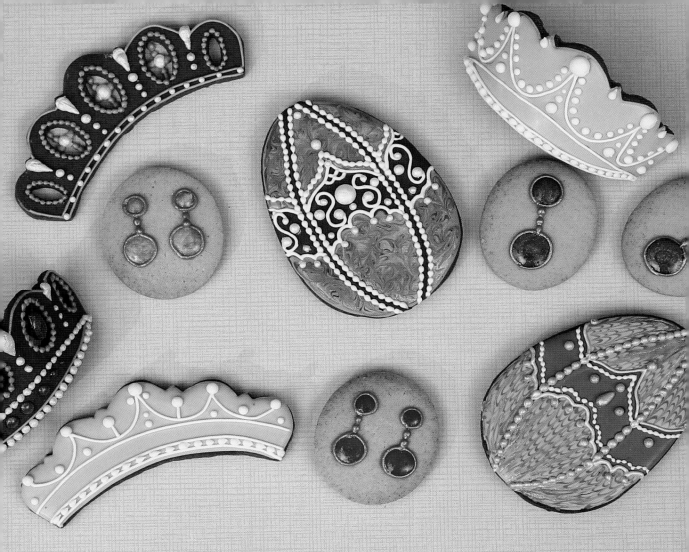

All that Glitters

Jewellery Biscuits

EDIBLES

Vanilla biscuit dough (see recipe on pages 12–13)

100g (3½oz) SK White Professional Instant Mix Royal Icing or Art-Ice Cookie Icing

SK Professional Liquid Food Colours: Chestnut, Rose, Sunflower

SK Designer Scintillo Piping Sparkles in your chosen colour

SK Classic Gold Designer Metallic Lustre Dust Food Colour

Clear alcohol, e.g. gin or vodka

EQUIPMENT

Essential equipment (see pages 8–9)

Oval biscuit cutters (measured lengthways): 45mm, 87mm (1³/₄", 3³/₈")

Small round plunger cutters: set of 3

Piping nozzle: no. 1.5

Makes approx. 12 large oval biscuits

Cutting out the biscuits

1 Prepare the biscuit dough following the recipe on pages 12–13 and colour it with two drops of Chestnut and one drop of Rose liquid food colour to give it a warm caramel tone.

TUTOR TIP

Add the liquid colour and any flavourings to the beaten egg rather than the finished dough.

2 Roll out the dough and cut out as many large oval biscuits as you can. Place on a lined baking tray then cut out the centre of each biscuit using the smaller oval cutter. Leave the centres on the tray – these will make the earring biscuits.

3 Lightly emboss the dough with round plunger cutters to mark out the gemstones. Use the largest cutter for the central stone and the smaller cutters towards the top of the biscuit. Mark two gems on the earring biscuits in the same way.

4 Bake the biscuits for 10–12 minutes following the recipe.

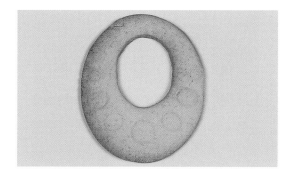

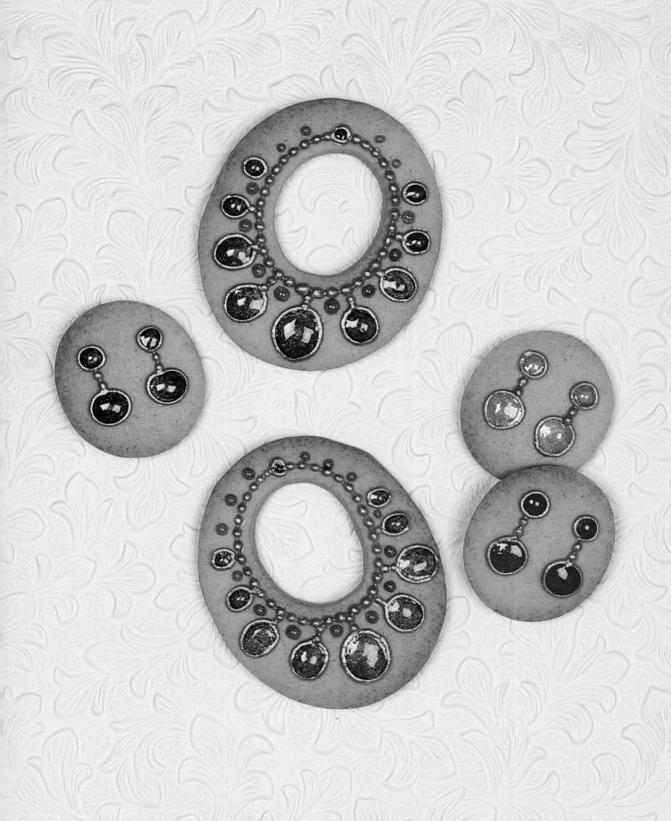

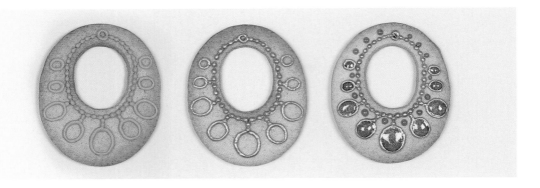

Making and colouring the icing

5 Shake the icing mix well and weigh out 100g (3½oz) into a bowl. Add 15ml (½fl oz) of cooled, boiled water and stir for approximately 5–10 minutes until it forms standing peaks (see page 17). Colour the icing with Chestnut and Sunflower liquid food colours to make a golden tone.

Decorating the biscuits

6 Place the no. 1.5 piping nozzle into a small piping bag and half-fill with the golden icing.

7 Pipe a running bead around the inside edge of the larger biscuits to make the necklace chain. Add running beads from the chain to the edge of the larger embossed gemstones. Outline each of the embossed circles with icing.

TOP TECHNIQUE

How to pipe a running bead: Touch the tip of the nozzle to the biscuit surface at a 45° angle and apply gentle pressure until you have piped a small bulb. Remove the pressure, slide the tip of the piping nozzle along slightly and repeat.

8 For the earrings, pipe a running bead between the two embossed gemstones then outline them as for the necklace. Set aside all the biscuits to dry completely.

9 Add a few drops of clear alcohol to a little Classic Gold lustre dust to make a thick paint. Brush the gold paint over all the piping.

TUTOR TIP

If the gold paint becomes too thick, add a few more drops of clear alcohol. If you get any gold paint on the biscuit, gently scrape it off with a scribing tool or the tip of a small, sharp knife.

10 Place the piping sparkles into a small piping bag and cut off the very tip of the bag. Fill each of the piped circles generously so that the gems appear domed.

11 Pipe some tiny gems in-between the larger gems and around the chain at the top of necklace. Allow to dry.

TUTOR TIP

If the piping sparkles are too runny to make a dome, fill the piping bag and leave it exposed to the air for several hours so the water evaporates and the gel thickens. The gel doesn't dry completely so avoid stacking the biscuits on top of one another when decorated.

Tiara Biscuits

EDIBLES

Light gingerbread dough (see recipe on page 14)

500g (1lb 1¾oz) SK Art-Ice Cookie Icing Mix

SK Rose Professional Liquid Food Colour

◆ ◆ ◆ ◆ ◆

Makes approx. 14 biscuits

EQUIPMENT

Essential equipment (see pages 8–9)

SK Crown Tiara Cookie Cutter

Ruler

Pizza cutter (optional)

Up to 14 clean, empty tin cans, approx. 8cm (3¹/₈")
in diameter

Aluminium foil

Piping nozzle: no. 1.5

Kitchen paper or non-slip matting

Cutting out the biscuits

1 Prepare the gingerbread dough following the recipe on page 14 and roll it out slightly thinner than usual. In order to stand upright the tiara biscuit needs a flat base, so use a ruler and a pizza cutter or sharp knife to cut a straight edge along the base of the rolled-out dough.

2 Position the tiara cutter so the lower points are touching this edge and press down on the top edge of the tiara only to cut through the dough. Remove the cutter, cut through any dough if necessary and place the biscuit, now with a straight lower edge, on a lined baking tray. Repeat to make as many biscuits as possible then chill in the fridge.

3 Preheat the oven at this stage then prepare the baking formers. Cut a strip of baking parchment wider than the tin and long enough to wrap around twice. Wrap the strip around the tin so that it overhangs at the open end, then tuck the excess paper into the tin to secure it in place. Take a strip of aluminium foil, roll up from each short end and place this on a baking tray first to prevent the tin from rolling off the baking sheet.

4 Balance a chilled tiara straight and centrally on the tin former and immediately place in the oven. As the dough warms up it will bend and bake to the shape of the tin.

5 Bake each biscuit for approximately 10–12 minutes. Leave the biscuit on the former for a couple of minutes before transferring to a rack to cool completely. If you are using the same former to bake another biscuit, allow it to cool before placing the next biscuit onto it.

Making and colouring the icing

6 Beat all the cookie icing mix with 75ml (2½oz) of cooled, boiled water until it forms standing peaks (see page 17) then follow the steps below rather than the pack instructions as they differ for curved biscuits.

7 Weigh out 100g (3½oz) of icing in a bowl for piping the decoration. Leave this icing white.

8 Colour the remaining icing with Rose liquid colour to make pink. Transfer 30g (1oz) of this icing to a separate bowl and set aside.

9 Add 20ml (¾fl oz) of cooled, boiled water to the remaining pink icing and mix gently. Test the consistency by drawing a clean knife across the top of the icing to leave a line: the line should disappear in 18–20 seconds. If it takes any longer than this add a few more drops of water and test again.

TUTOR TIP

Where the whole curved biscuit is coated, a thicker than usual run-out icing is required to prevent it running off the edge of the biscuit. Dividing the biscuit into sections also helps to achieve an even coating.

Decorating the biscuits

10 Place a piece of non-slip mat or kitchen roll onto the paper-wrapped tin can to support the biscuit while it is being decorated and prevent it falling off. Wedge the tin between the foil pieces and turn when necessary so you are working on the top rather than the side of the biscuits where possible.

11 Fit a small piping bag with a no. 1.5 nozzle and half-fill with the thick, pink piping icing. Following the step pictures, pipe the outline along the top of the biscuit, the internal curved lines, and finally the line across the base.

TUTOR TIP

If you wish you can use a food colour pen to draw guidelines on the biscuit to follow when piping the outlines (see page 49).

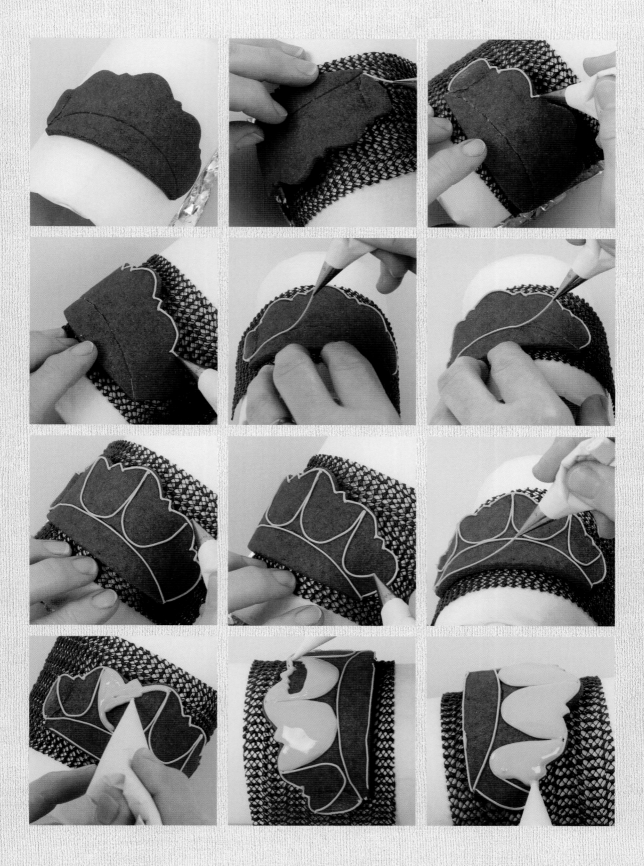

 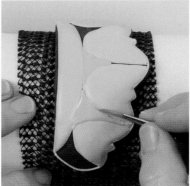 

12 Half-fill a paper piping bag with the pink run-out icing, cut a small hole in the tip and fill the top sections of the tiara, starting with the two in the centre. Note that the icing is not piped to the lowest edge on the outside sections, gravity will pull the icing to the edge and you can help it along by teasing the icing down with the tip of the bag.

13 Fill the long crescent shape and use a slightly damp paintbrush to ease the icing into the corners. Set aside to dry for 10 minutes or so.

14 Fill the remaining areas with the pink run-out icing. Where there is a very narrow section to fill, squash the end of the bag flat before filling and use a paintbrush to ease the icing into the corners. Set aside to dry completely.

15 Fit a small piping bag with a no. 1.5 nozzle and half-fill with the thick, white icing. Drop lines over any joins between the pink run-out sections and then embellish by piping pearls and running beads alongside the lines. Allow to dry completely.

Alternative designs

The designs on page 63 and opposite show that is isn't always necessary to completely coat the biscuit – you can still achieve opulent results leaving the biscuit 'bare' and adding some piped embellishments.

Gold and white tiara: tip a pot of SK Classic Gold Metallic Lustre Dust into a small muslin square, gather the four corners together and tie with string or ribbon to make a dusting bag. Once all the biscuits are cut out, thickly dust all the raw dough using a firm dabbing action with the bag. Bake the biscuits and allow to cool. Make up 200g (7oz) of cookie icing or royal icing and pipe a design using drop lines and pearls. Once the icing has dried, add a little sparkle to the pearls by dropping piping gel on top.

Emerald and gold: use small geometric cutters to cut out oval or round shapes from the biscuit dough while it is lying flat. Cut out extra shapes from the dough, a size smaller, to form the gems. Bake all of the biscuit pieces then decorate when cool. Pipe running beads, pearls and drop lines in white piping icing, then colour with gold metallic paint when dry. Lightly grease a piece of cellophane onto the former and put the curved biscuit on top. Pipe four large pearls equally around each cut-out piece and drop in one of the tiny biscuits. Once dry, cover the tiny biscuit with Scintillo piping sparkles in green or your choice of colour.

Flat tiaras: for a simpler design, bake the tiaras flat and decorate with either a combination of run-out and piping icing or gold lustre dust and piping icing. If you're making flat biscuits you won't need to trim the bottom straight.

Fabergé Egg Biscuits

EDIBLES

Chocolate biscuit dough (see recipe on pages 12–13)

500g (1lb 1¾oz) SK Art-ice Cookie Icing Mix

SK Black Food Colour Pen

SK Purple Quality Food Colour (QFC) Liquid

SK Quality Food Colour (QFC) Dusts: Pearl, Purple

Clear alcohol, e.g. gin or vodka

EQUIPMENT

Essential equipment (see pages 8–9)

SK Easter Egg Cookie Cutter

Piping nozzles: nos. 1, 1.5

Sheet of coloured card, ruler and pencil

Piece of thin card (any colour)

15cm (6") square cake drum

SK Paintbrush: no. 4

Template (see page 123)

◆ ◆ ◆ ◆ ◆

Makes approx. 12 biscuits

Cutting out the biscuits

1 Prepare and roll out the chocolate biscuit dough following the recipe on pages 12–13. Cut out 12 egg-shaped biscuits using the cutter, place on a lined baking tray and bake for approximately 10–12 minutes.

Making and colouring the icing

2 Beat all the cookie icing mix with 75ml (2½oz) of cooled, boiled water until it forms standing peaks (see page 17). Weigh out 60g (2oz) of piping icing into a separate bowl. Add 45ml (1½oz) of cooled, boiled water to the remainder of the icing to make run-out icing (see page 17).

3 Divide the thick piping icing equally between two bowls. Colour the icing in one bowl a rich purple using a mixture of purple liquid and dust food colours and leave the second bowl white.

4 Fit a small piping bag with a no. 1.5 nozzle and half-fill with the purple icing.

5 Weigh out 200g (7oz) of the run-out icing into another bowl and colour it a very pale shade of purple. Colour another 100g (3½oz) of run-out icing very dark purple and leave the remaining icing white.

6 Half-fill three medium piping bags with the pale purple, dark purple and white run-out icing respectively and snip a small hole in the tip (or use icing bottles if you prefer).

Making the pearls

7 Use a ruler and pencil to draw a series of parallel lines ranging from 2mm–5mm ($\frac{1}{16}$"–$\frac{1}{4}$") apart on a piece of coloured card. Place the card on a cake drum and trim it down so it sits well within the edge of the drum. Cover with cellophane and secure at the corners with tape. Lightly grease the cellophane with white vegetable fat.

8 Use the white run-out icing to pipe lots of small dots between the lines. Leave for up to 24 hours so they dry completely; in the meantime you can decorate the biscuits.

Decorating the biscuits

9 Copy the template onto a piece of thin card then use a black food colour pen to draw guidelines onto the biscuits.

10 Use the thick purple piping icing with the no. 1.5 nozzle to pipe the inverted 'V'-shaped lines in the centre of the oval first, then pipe two parallel rows of long, curved lines down each side of the oval, keeping the lines very close together. Add the horizontal lines on either side then finish by outlining the biscuit.

11 Pipe the dark purple run-out icing into one of the outside sections of the egg and repeat on the opposite side.

12 Make a thin mix of the pearl dust food colour and clear alcohol in a paint palette or saucer. Fill in the lower central area with pale purple run-out icing then immediately drop in random squiggles and dots with the dark purple run-out icing. Dip the paintbrush into the pearl paint and use this to mix the two colours together in a swirling motion. If necessary, wipe off any excess icing and refresh the brush with more pearl paint until the whole area is pearlescent.

13 Repeat step 12 to fill in the top central area. Allow to dry for 5–10 minutes under a lamp.

14 Use the dark purple run-out icing to fill the very central area.

15 Repeat step 12 for the other four outside sections of the egg then set aside to dry fully.

16 Use the thick purple icing to pipe a single line between the two sets of parallel lines.

17 Fit a small piping bag with a no. 1 nozzle and half-fill with the thick white piping icing. Over-pipe the join between the dark and marbled sections with lines, running beads and scallops. Pipe small pearls directly onto the egg.

18 Save the remaining white piping icing for attaching the pearls and store it overnight (see page 17).

Attaching the pearls

19 Once the pearls have dried, mix the pearl lustre dust and a few drops of clear alcohol together to make a paint. Use a no. 4 paintbrush to paint the dried pearls with the mixture and set aside until ready to use.

20 Fit a small piping bag with a no. 1 piping nozzle and half-fill with the reserved white piping icing. Using the pictures for guidance pipe a series of S and C shapes in the central sections.

21 Release the pre-prepared pearls from the cellophane by giving them a gentle push with your fingertip, then attach them to the biscuit with small dots of icing.

22 Pipe a running bead down each side of the long purple lines to finish.

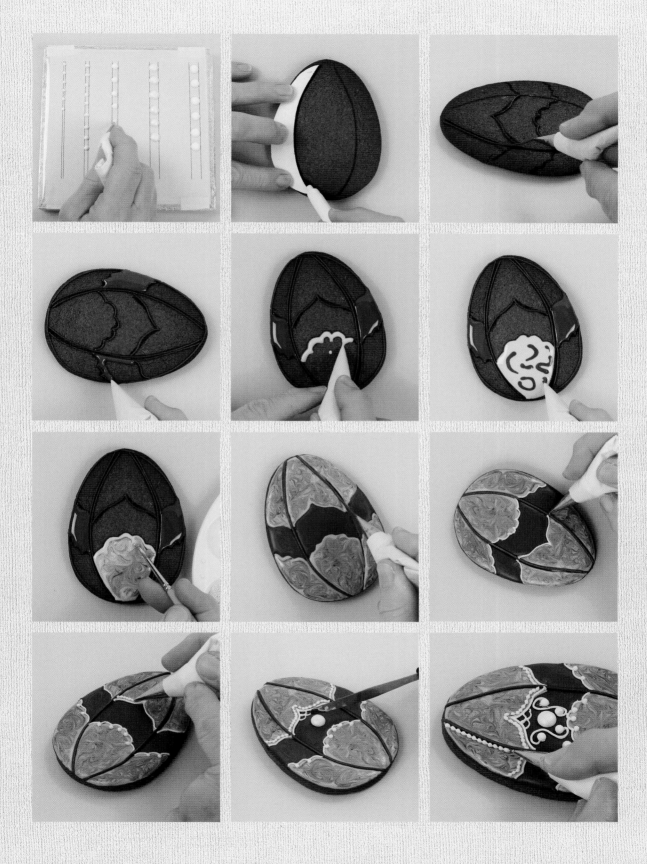

Alternative designs

These variations on the purple design are achieved in the same way using different colours.

Turquoise egg: colour the icing in shades of Hydrangea liquid food colour and brush the piped decoration silver using a mixture of lustre dust and clear alcohol.

Green egg: colour the icing with SK Dark Green liquid food colour and brush the embellishments using a mixture of Classic Gold lustre dust and clear alcohol.

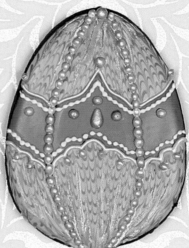

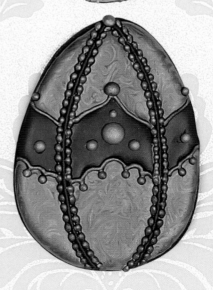

Hobbies

Pool Balls

EDIBLES

Vanilla biscuit dough (see recipe on pages 12–13)

500g (1lb 1¾oz) SK Art-Ice Cookie Icing Mix

SK Food Colour Pens: Black, Orange

SK Professional Liquid Food Colours: Bulrush, Chestnut, Daffodil, Hyacinth, Poinsettia, Violet

SK Quality Food Colour (QFC) Dust: Black

EQUIPMENT

Essential equipment (see pages 8–9)

5cm (2") round cookie cutter

7 small bowls

Piping nozzle: no. 1.5

Template (see page 123)

Thin card

Makes 32 biscuits (2 sets of pool balls)

Cutting out the biscuits

1 Prepare and roll out the vanilla biscuit dough following the recipe on pages 12–13. Cut out 32 biscuits using the round cutter, then bake the biscuits for 7–8 minutes.

Making and colouring the icing

2 Beat all the cookie icing mix with 75ml (2½oz) of cooled, boiled water until it forms standing peaks (see page 17). Weigh out 60g (2oz) of piping icing into a separate bowl. Add 45ml (1½oz) of cooled, boiled water to the remainder of the icing to make run-out icing (see page 17).

3 Colour the thick piping icing to a pale biscuit colour using Chestnut liquid food colour. Fit a small piping bag with a no. 1.5 nozzle and half-fill with the pale brown icing.

4 Weigh out 20g (¾oz) of the run-out icing into a bowl and colour with Black dust. Take a further four bowls, weigh out 40g (1½oz) into each bowl and colour with Poinsettia, Hyacinth, Violet and Bulrush liquid food colours respectively. Weigh 80g (2¾oz) into another bowl and colour with Daffodil. Leave the remaining run-out icing white. Place the white and each colour into medium paper piping bags with no nozzle.

Decorating the biscuits

5 Copy the pool ball template onto thin card. Set aside two biscuits then use the orange food colour pen to draw the small circle onto the remaining biscuits. Draw the two outer curves on 14 of the biscuits.

6 Use the light brown piping icing to pipe over the circles and outer curves where marked and outline each biscuit.

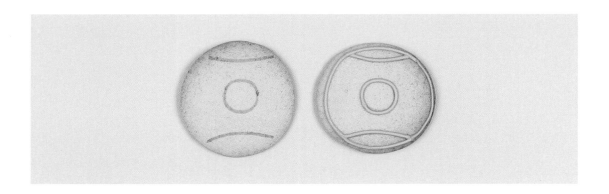

7 Fill the pool ball with colour first and then the white circle and outer curves where needed. Use the tip of the piping bag to ease the white and colour to just touch each other. While the coloured icing is still wet, pipe two small dots of white icing on either side of the white circle, put the tip of a scriber into the centre and pull to one side to make a reflective shine. Set aside to dry completely.

8 Coat two biscuits with white icing only and allow to dry.

Finishing the biscuits

9 Once the icing is dry use the black food colour pen to write the number on each of the coloured and black balls.

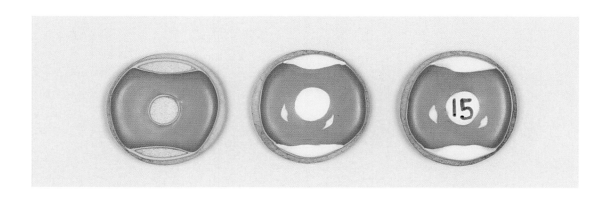

Compass Biscuits

EDIBLES

Light gingerbread dough (see recipe on page 14)

200g (7oz) SK White Professional Instant Mix Royal Icing or Art-Ice Cookie Icing

SK Professional Liquid Food Colours: Chestnut, Daffodil, Hyacinth, Lilac, Poinsettia

SK Classic Gold Designer Metallic Lustre Dust Food Colour

Clear alcohol, e.g. vodka or gin

SK Black Food Colour Pen

EQUIPMENT

Essential equipment (see pages 8–9)

Round cookie cutters: 6cm, 9cm (2³/₈", 3¹/₂")

Piping nozzles: nos. 1, 2, 3

Template (see page 123)

Makes approx. 8 biscuits

Cutting out the biscuits

1 Prepare and roll out the gingerbread dough following the recipe on page 14. Cut out eight biscuits using the 9cm (3½") round cutter, place on a lined baking tray then use the 6cm (2³⁄₈") cutter to emboss a ring on each biscuit. Bake the biscuits for approximately 10–12 minutes.

TUTOR TIP

Lean directly over the biscuit when embossing the ring to ensure it is central.

Making and colouring the icing

2 Weigh out 200g (7oz) of the cookie icing mix, add 30ml (1fl oz) of cooled, boiled water and stir vigorously until thick. Remove a tablespoon of the thick icing. Add 2–3tsp of cooled, boiled water to the remainder to make the run-out icing (see page 17).

3 Divide the thick piping icing in half and colour one batch dark Bulrush and the other Chestnut.

4 Place a tablespoon of run-out icing into each of five bowls and colour with Daffodil, Chestnut, Hyacinth, Lilac and Poinsettia.

Decorating the biscuits

5 Cut the template out of thin card. Place it within the central circle of each biscuit and draw around the shape with the black food colour pen.

6 Fit a small piping bag with a no. 1 piping nozzle and half-fill with the dark brown piping icing. Pipe over the marked central design.

7 Half-fill small piping bags with the yellow, blue, red and lilac run-out icing and fill the largest points. Set aside to dry for 5–10 minutes.

8 Mix together blue and yellow run-out icing to make green; yellow and red icing to make orange; red and lilac icing to make burgundy; and lilac and blue icing to make indigo. Place these colours into small piping bags and fill the intermediate points on each compass, using a fine paintbrush to ease the icing into the points. Set aside to dry for 10 minutes and save the remaining orange icing for later.

9 Fit a small piping bag with a no. 3 nozzle and half-fill with the thick Chestnut piping icing. Pipe over the embossed circle on the biscuits.

10 Fit a small piping bag with a no. 2 nozzle and half-fill with the Chestnut piping icing. Pipe the letters around the outer edge of the compass. Fill the central circle with the reserved orange run-out icing. Set aside to dry completely.

11 Mix some gold lustre dust with clear alcohol to make a thin paste and paint the letters, central circle and ring on the compass using a fine paintbrush.

TUTOR TIP

The dark colour of the gingerbread is an excellent background for the bright colours of this compass design and makes it unnecessary to fully coat the biscuits.

Vinyl Records

EDIBLES

Chocolate biscuit dough (see recipe on pages 12–13)

250g (8¾oz) SK Tuxedo Black Professional Instant Mix Royal Icing

200g (7oz) SK Art-Ice Cookie Icing Mix

SK Professional Liquid Food Colours: Bluebell, Daffodil, Mint, Nasturtium

SK Silver Designer Metallic Lustre Dust Food Colour

Clear alcohol, e.g. vodka or gin

EQUIPMENT

Essential equipment (see pages 8–9)

Round cookie cutters: 4cm, 9cm (1½", 3½")

Small round plunger cutters: set of 3

Piping nozzles: no. 1.5, 5 x no. 2 (or use piping bottles), no. 3

Small square or oblong cake drum

Makes approx. 12 records

Cutting out the biscuits

1 Prepare and roll out the chocolate biscuit dough following the recipe on pages 12–13. Cut out 12 vinyl records using the 9cm (3½") round cutter and place on the lined baking sheet, leaving plenty of space between each one.

2 Use the 4cm (1½") cookie cutter to emboss a circle centrally on each biscuit, pressing gently to leave a faint mark. Use the medium-sized plunger cutter from the set to cut out the centre of each biscuit.

3 Bake the biscuits for approximately 10–12 minutes.

Making and colouring the icing

4 Shake the bag of black royal icing well and sift out 250g (8¾oz) into a bowl. Add 35ml (1¼fl oz) of cooled, boiled water and stir vigorously for 5–10 minutes until the icing is thick. Fit a medium piping bag with a no. 3 nozzle and half-fill with the black piping icing.

5 Shake the bag of cookie icing mix and sift out 200g (7oz) into a bowl. Add 30ml (1fl oz) of cooled, boiled water and stir vigorously for 5–10 minutes until the icing is thick. Remove a couple of teaspoons of the thick white icing for outlining the record player arm and set aside. Add 3–4tsp of cooled, boiled water to the remaining icing and stir gently to make a run-out consistency (see page 17).

6 Divide the thin run-out icing between five small bowls. Leave one bowl white and tint the others with Bluebell, Daffodil, Mint and Nasturtium liquid food colours. Fill icing bottles or plastic piping bags fitted with no. 2 nozzles.

TUTOR TIP

When colouring a small amount of icing to a pastel colour, even a single drop of colouring may be too much. Instead, dip a paintbrush into the opening of the bottle and use this to transfer colour into the icing. Repeat until the required tint is achieved.

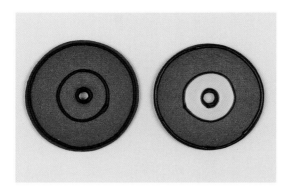

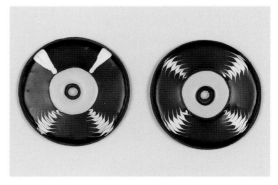

Decorating the biscuits

7 Use the black piping icing to outline the records. Start by outlining the central hole and then work outwards.

8 Return the black icing to the bowl and add 3–4tsp of cooled, boiled water to make a thin run-out icing. Fill an icing bottle or piping bag fitted with a no. 2 nozzle.

9 Fill the central label area of the vinyl records with the different pastel-coloured run-out icing and set aside to dry for at least 30 minutes.

10 Half-fill a medium piping bag with white run-out icing and cut a small hole in the tip.

11 Fill the first vinyl record with black run-out icing and immediately drop in narrow wedge shapes of white run-out icing. Place the tip of a scriber into the centre and pull to one side, then clean the scriber, place the tip into the centre just below the first line and pull to the opposite side. Continue down the length of the white line, cleaning the scriber each time.

12 Continue to create the other white lines on each record in the same way then set aside to dry completely.

13 To make the record player arm, place the template on a small cake drum, cover with cellophane and lightly grease with white vegetable fat. Outline with white piping icing and a no. 1.5 nozzle. Fill the arm with white run-out icing, allow to dry for 5–10 minutes and then fill the head. Allow to dry completely.

14 Mix a little silver lustre dust with clear alcohol and paint the arm. Make as many as required then allow to dry completely. Attach to the biscuits with a small amount of royal icing.

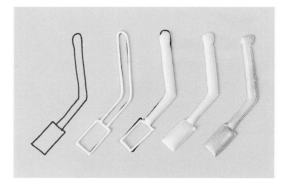

TUTOR TIP

You can personalise the records by writing the recipient's favourite song on the label. Use a fine-tipped black food colour pen or black liquid food colour and a fine paintbrush.

Flying High

Buzzy Bees

EDIBLES

Vanilla biscuit dough (see recipe on pages 12–13)

250g (8¾oz) SK Art-Ice Cookie Icing Mix

200g (7oz) SK Tuxedo Black Professional Instant Mix Royal Icing

SK Professional Liquid Food Colours: Chestnut, Sunflower

SK Orange Food Colour Pen

Clear alcohol, e.g. vodka or gin

SK Piping Gel

EQUIPMENT

Essential equipment (see pages 8–9)

Bumblebee cookie cutter

Piping nozzle: no. 1.5

Makes 24 biscuits

Cutting out the biscuits

1 Prepare and roll out the vanilla biscuit dough following the recipe on pages 12–13. Cut out 24 biscuits using the bee cutter then place on a lined baking tray and bake them for approximately 7–8 minutes. Allow to cool.

Making and colouring the icing

2 Beat 250g of the cookie icing mix with 35ml (1¼fl oz) of cooled, boiled water until it forms standing peaks (see page 17). Weigh out 30g (1oz) of piping icing into a separate bowl. Add 20ml (¾fl oz) of cooled, boiled water to the remainder of the icing to make a thin run-out consistency (see page 17).

3 Colour the thick piping icing with Chestnut liquid food colour to make a pale biscuit colour. Fit a small piping bag with a no. 1.5 nozzle and half-fill with the biscuit-coloured icing.

4 Divide the thin run-out icing between two bowls and colour one with Sunflower liquid food colour. Leave the other bowl white. Half-fill two medium paper piping bags with the run-out icings.

5 Sift 200g (7oz) of black royal icing mix into a bowl and add 30ml (1fl oz) of cooled, boiled water. Stir vigorously until the icing is stiff. Add a small amount of cooled, boiled water to thin the icing to run-out consistency. Half-fill a medium piping bag with no nozzle.

Decorating the biscuits

6 Use the orange food colour pen to draw the bee wings on each biscuit. Outline the wings and the bee's body with the biscuit-coloured piping icing.

7 Snip the tip off the bags of black and yellow run-out icing. Pipe black run-out icing at the top of the bee's

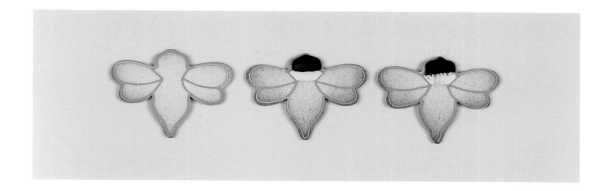

head, then immediately pipe a band of yellow icing below. Blend the two icings slightly by dragging the very tip of a scribing tool or cocktail stick from the edge of the black icing into the yellow icing to create a hair-like effect. Continue across the width of the head, wiping the scribing tool or cocktail stick clean with a damp cloth when needed.

8 Pipe a band of black icing under the yellow and repeat the dragging technique in step 7.

9 Pipe another band of yellow icing under the black and finish with black at the tip. Continue to blend the colours as described in step 7. Repeat on all of the biscuits then aside to dry for at least half an hour.

10 Mix a few drops of Chestnut liquid food colour with one or two drops of clear alcohol to thin it.

11 Snip the tip off the bag of white run-out icing and fill the top half of the wings. While the icing is still wet, dip the tip of the scriber into the Chestnut colour and pull it through the wet icing to form the veins on the wings. Set aside to dry for 5–10 minutes.

12 Repeat step 11 for the lower half of the wings. Set aside to dry completely.

13 Put 2tsp of piping gel into a small, heatproof bowl and heat in a microwave on full power until it bubbles up. Carefully remove the bowl and immediately paint the gel over the wings to give them a gloss.

TUTOR TIP

To avoid colour bleeding where a very pale colour is to be piped adjacent to a very strong colour, such as white next to black, allow one area to dry well before filling the next one.

Blue Tit Biscuits

EDIBLES

Vanilla biscuit dough (see recipe on pages 12–13)

500g (1lb 1¾oz) SK Art-Ice Cookie Icing Mix

SK Professional Liquid Food Colours: Chestnut, Daffodil, Hyacinth

SK Black Quality Food Colour (QFC) Dust

SK Orange Food Colour Pen

EQUIPMENT

Essential equipment (see pages 8–9)

SK Dove Cookie Cutter

Piping nozzle: no. 1.5

4 x piping bottles with no. 1.5 nozzles (optional)

Makes approx. 10 biscuits

Cutting out the biscuits

1 Prepare and roll out the vanilla biscuit dough following the recipe on pages 12–13. Cut out approximately 10 biscuits using the dove cutter then place on a lined baking tray and bake them for approximately 10–12 minutes. Allow to cool.

Making and colouring the icing

2 Beat all the cookie icing mix with 75ml (2½oz) of cooled, boiled water until it forms standing peaks (see page 17). Weigh out 60g (2oz) of piping icing into a separate bowl. Add 45ml (1½oz) of cooled, boiled water to the remainder of the icing to make run-out icing (see page 17).

3 Colour the thick piping icing with Chestnut liquid food colour to match the biscuits. Fit a small piping bag with a no. 1.5 nozzle and half-fill with the light brown icing.

4 Divide and colour the run-out icing as follows: 100g (3½oz) with Daffodil to make yellow, 280g (9¾oz) with Hyacinth to make bright blue, 25g (just under 1oz) black, and leave the remainder white. Add a touch of the blue icing to the yellow to give a slight green tinge. Place 160g (5½oz) of the blue icing into a clean bowl and add a small amount of black dust, making a darker tone to contrast with the bright blue.

Decorating the biscuits

5 Use the orange food pen to sketch out where the different colours are to be placed on the bird.

6 Use the light brown piping icing to outline the back wing and the body/front wing of the bird.

7 Put the bright blue, darker blue and yellow run-out icing each into a medium piping bag with no nozzle or piping bottle fitted with a no. 1.5 nozzle. Place the white and black run-out icing each into a small piping bag then cut a very small hole into the tip of each piping bag.

TUTOR TIP

The shading and patterns are all created with the wet-in-wet technique, so make sure all your piping bags are filled and ready to be used before you start piping.

8 Start on the back wing and use the bright blue icing to fill from the body line to about $^2/_3$ up the wing. Fill the remaining area with the darker blue shade. Pipe two thin black lines at the point where the two blue icings meet and a few lines or dots at the wing base. Use a scriber to pull from the base through the dots and lines to blend the colours, then pull the scriber through the double lines so the markings are feathered. If necessary mix up the black and blue slightly more at the base. Set aside to dry for 10 minutes.

9 The main body of the bird is piped from the top of the head down the body and wing to the tail with no drying time between the different coloured areas. Start by piping a bright blue cap on the top of the head.

10 Outline the beak with black run-out icing, tapering the icing at the point. Fill the gap between the black lines with a thin line of white run-out icing.

11 Pipe directly underneath the blue cap with a white stripe and then a further bright blue stripe, leaving a gap for the eye. Drop in a dot of black icing for the eye, highlighting with a tiny drop of white. Pipe the white throat.

12 Add an area of bright blue under the throat and down towards the chest. Drop a small triangle of black under the edge of the white throat. Pipe a stripe of white and then yellow at the start of the wing.

13 Fill about half of the wing with the bright blue and the remaining area with dark blue. Drop lines and dots of black along the base of the wing and two lines across the join of the two blues. Use the scriber to blend the black at the base of the wing and feather the line by pulling the scriber from the bright blue area through to the tip of the wing. Pipe dashes of white under the feathered black line.

14 Fill in the chest area with yellow then blend the join between the blue and yellow by breaking the line with the scriber. Pipe a line of bright blue at the base of the yellow chest and use the scriber to draw very small and random dashes in the yellow towards the outer edge of the biscuit.

15 Continue the bright blue along the top edge of the tail and fill the remaining area of the tail with dark blue. Pipe a line of black along the join then blend the join between the yellow and blue and feather across the black line, taking the scriber to the tip of the tail to bring the dark colour right to the edge. On some of the birds drop a small triangle of white under the yellow. Set aside to dry fully.

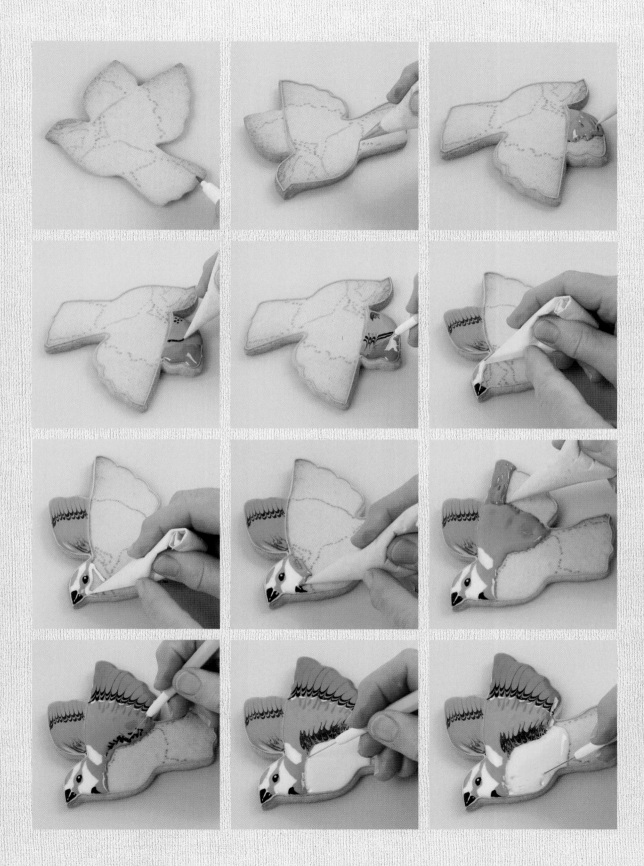

Butterfly Biscuits

EDIBLES

Light gingerbread dough (see recipe on page 14)

500g (1lb 1¾oz) SK Art-Ice Cookie Icing Mix

SK Professional Liquid Food Colours: Berberis, Bulrush, Poppy

SK Black Quality Food Colour (QFC) Liquid

SK Black Food Colour Pen

EQUIPMENT

Essential equipment (see pages 8–9)

SK Large Butterfly Cookie Cutter

Piping nozzles: nos. 1.5, 3

Small square or oblong cake board

6 small round or square cake boards

Sheet of card, any pale colour

Small oblongs of food-grade sponge

Makes 6 large biscuits

Cutting out the biscuits

1 Prepare and roll out the gingerbread dough following the recipe on page 14. Cut out six large butterfly biscuits then place on a lined baking tray and bake them for approximately 10–12 minutes.

2 As soon as you have taken the biscuits out of the oven, cut each biscuit in half to separate the wings. Transfer to a wire cooling rack and allow to go cold.

Making and colouring the icing

3 Beat all the cookie icing mix with 75ml (2½oz) of cooled, boiled water until it forms standing peaks (see page 17) then follow the steps below rather than the pack instructions.

4 Weigh out 100g (3½oz) of the thick piping icing and colour with Bulrush liquid food colour to make dark

brown. Half-fill a small piping bag fitted with a no. 1.5 nozzle with the icing and cover the rest until required.

5 Add 40ml (1½fl oz) of cooled, boiled water to the remaining white icing to make a run-out consistency. Divide and colour the run-out icing as follows: 150g (5¼oz) black, 100g (3½oz) with Bulrush to make dark brown, and 100g (3½oz) with Poppy and a touch of Berberis to make red. Leave the remainder of the icing white. Half-fill medium paper piping bags with each of the colours then, when you're ready to use each one, cut off the tip.

Decorating the biscuits

6 Draw lines onto the wings as a guideline for the decoration using a black food colour pen. This will help to ensure that each pair of wings is symmetrical.

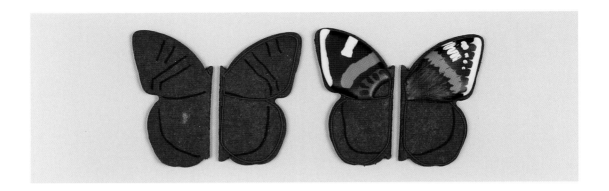

7 Cut a piece of card smaller than the cake board then cut a piece of cellophane to the same size and attach firmly at the corners with masking tape. Grease the cellophane very lightly with white vegetable fat.

8 Using the bag of thick, dark brown piping icing, pipe a short line with a bulb of icing at the end onto the prepared cellophane to represent the antennae. These are fragile so pipe twice as many as required to finish the butterflies. Allow to dry fully.

9 Use the same piping bag to outline the butterfly wings.

10 Starting on the outside edge of the upper wing, pipe black and white run-out icing over the markings to just above where the red diagonal stripe will be, following the pictures for guidance. Use a scriber to blend the icing then pull the tip of the scriber from one colour into another to create a feathered effect. You can mix the colours by making tiny clockwise and anti-clockwise circles in the different coloured icings.

11 Continue working down the wing by piping a broad red stripe, a line of black and then dark brown, marking with a scriber as you go. Leave the very inside corner of the wing empty as this will fill as the icing is pulled down.

TUTOR TIP

Work on one pair of wings at a time so the markings match as closely as possible but fill and mark one wing at a time while the icing is still wet.

TUTOR TIP

When manipulating icing in this way it is slowly dragged to the finishing point and there can be a build-up of icing. To prevent this leave an empty area at the finishing point where the icing can spread into.

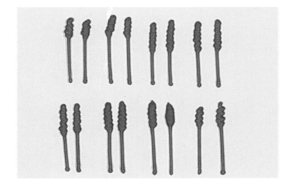

12 Immediately fill and mark the top of the opposite wing, matching them as closely as possible. Set aside to dry for 5–10 minutes.

13 Fill and mark the lower part of the wings following the same method as for the top part, starting from the outer edge and working inwards. Set the wings aside to dry fully.

Assembling the butterflies

14 Cover a small cake board with cellophane, secure in place with masking tape and lightly grease with white vegetable fat.

15 Fit a medium piping bag with a no. 3 nozzle and half-fill with the reserved dark brown piping icing. Pipe a 3cm (1⅛") long line on the greased cellophane and place an oblong of sponge either side.

16 Place a pair of wings into the icing and move the sponge pieces until the wings are at a pleasing angle.

17 Starting just below the top of the biscuit, use the bag of dark brown piping icing to pipe three or four elongated bulbs of icing. On the last bulb pull the icing bag away from the butterfly while reducing pressure to create a tapering point. Pipe a large pearl for the head of the butterfly and immediately push in two antennae – these can be released from the cellophane carefully by pushing gently with your fingertip. Set aside to dry fully.

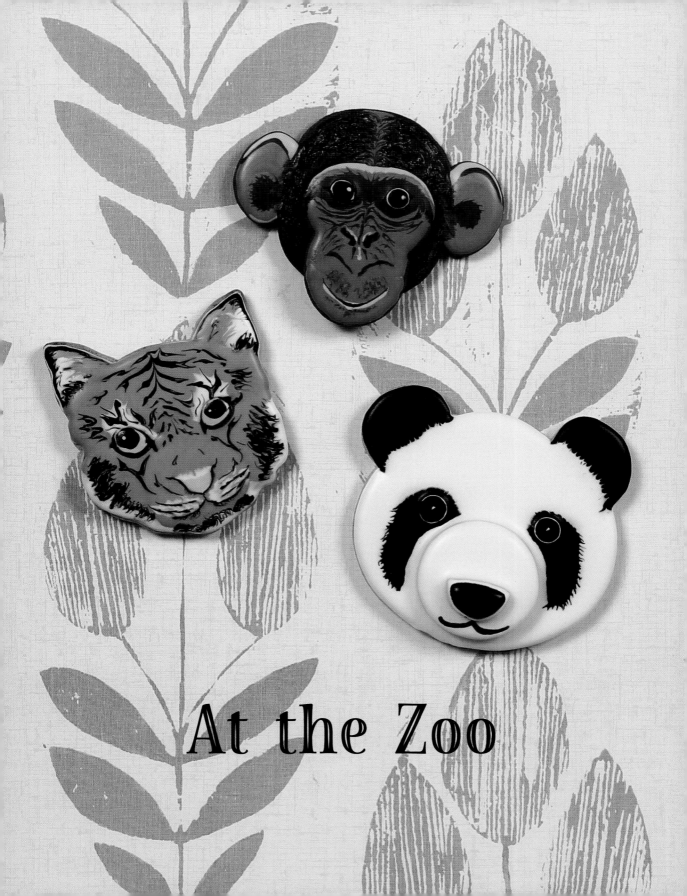

At the Zoo

Panda

EDIBLES

Vanilla biscuit dough (see recipe on pages 12–13)

500g (1lb 1¾oz) SK Art-Ice Cookie Icing Mix

100g (3½oz) SK Tuxedo Black Professional Instant Mix Royal Icing

SK Black Food Colour Pen

EQUIPMENT

Essential equipment (see pages 8–9)

Teddy bear face cookie cutter, approximately 9.5cm x 11cm (3¾" x 4¼") in size

Round cookie cutters: 2.5cm, 5cm (1", 2")

Piping nozzle: no. 1.5

2 piping bottles with no. 2 nozzles

Makes approx. 10 biscuits

Cutting out the biscuits

1 Prepare the vanilla biscuit dough following the recipe on pages 12–13, roll out and cut out 10 teddy bear heads. These cuddly pandas are given extra dimension by using layers of biscuits to create the muzzle and nose: cut out 10 x 5cm (2") round biscuits for the muzzles then cut out five 2.5cm (1") round biscuits and cut them in half for the noses. Place these smaller biscuits in the centre of the baking tray with the heads around the edge.

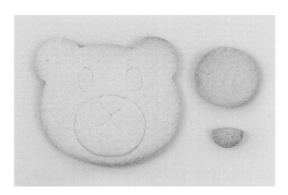

2 Bake the biscuits for 10–12 minutes following the recipe.

TUTOR TIP

If you're using a teddy cookie cutter that embosses the muzzle and eyes onto the biscuits, ignore the markings when decorating the panda face.

Making and colouring the icing

3 Beat all the cookie icing mix with 75ml (2½oz) of cooled, boiled water until it forms standing peaks (see page 17). Weigh out 60g (2oz) of piping icing into a separate bowl. Add 45ml (1½oz) of cooled, boiled water to the remainder of the icing to make run-out icing (see page 17).

4 To make up the black icing, shake the bag well and measure out 100g (3½oz) of royal icing powder into a clean bowl. Add 15ml (3tsp) of cooled, boiled water and stir vigorously for 5–10 minutes until the icing is thick. Gently stir in a further 1–2tsp of water until the black icing is a similar consistency to the white run-out icing.

Decorating the biscuits

5 Place a no. 1.5 nozzle into a small piping bag and half-fill with white piping icing. Squeeze a little icing onto the back of the small semicircle biscuit and fix to the round biscuit as shown in the picture. Squeeze a little icing onto the back of the round biscuit and position it towards the bottom of the face.

6 Use the same bag of white piping icing to pipe over-sized pearls on each side of the muzzle to make the eyes.

7 Outline the biscuit using the white piping icing, starting at the corner of one ear.

8 Place the black and white run-out icings into the piping bottles with no. 2 nozzles, or piping bags with the tip snipped off. Fill the ears with black, carefully covering the white outline. The icing can be teased over the line with a slightly damp paintbrush if needed.

9 Immediately fill the forehead area with white run-out icing and blend the join towards the ear with a scriber.

10 Pipe a line of black run-out icing around the eyes and continue outwards to make a lozenge shape, leaving a gap between the head and muzzle biscuits. Bring the white icing around the eyes and onto the cheeks.

11 Outline the nose with white run-out icing (don't fill in the top) and use the tip of the bottle or nozzle to encourage it to trickle down the side of the small biscuit. Continue onto the muzzle area, again encouraging the icing to coat the edge of the biscuit. If necessary neaten the area between the muzzle and the black eye patches.

12 Use a scriber to pull the white icing into the black icing, starting just outside the black area and working inwards.

TUTOR TIP

The markings on the face are made while both the black and white icings are wet so they can be blended to give a furry effect. After pulling the scriber from the white into the black areas make sure you wipe it clean otherwise it will mark the white icing next time you pull it through.

13 Fill the chin area with white run-out icing.

14 Fill the centre of the nose with black run-out icing. Complete one biscuit at a time then set them aside to dry fully.

15 To finish the faces use the edible food colour pen to draw on a smile and colour in the eyes, leaving a small dot of white in the centre.

TUTOR TIP

You can give your pandas different coloured eyes using different food pens – both brown and dark blue work very well.

Chimpanzee

EDIBLES

Chocolate biscuit dough (see recipe on pages 12–13)

500g (1lb 1¾oz) SK Art-Ice Cookie Icing Mix

SK Professional Liquid Food Colours: Bulrush, Nasturtium

SK Black Quality Food Colour (QFC) Liquid

SK Black Food Colour Pen

EQUIPMENT

Essential equipment (see pages 8–9)

Round cookie cutters: 7.5cm, 8.5cm (3", 3³/₈")

Oval cookie cutters: 3.5cm, 4.7cm (1³/₈", 2")

5.5cm (2¼") heart cookie cutter

Piping nozzles: no. 1.5, 2 x no. 3

Makes approx. 8 biscuits

Cutting out the biscuits

1 Prepare the chocolate biscuit dough following the recipe on pages 12–13, roll out and cut out the following shapes for each chimp face: 1 x 7.5cm (3") round, 1 x 4.7cm (2") oval, 2 x 3.5cm (1³/₈") ovals, and 1 x 5.5cm (2¼") heart .

TUTOR TIP

This cheeky chimp is decorated as two biscuits which are then fixed together. This not only gives the face more of a profile but means you can work on smaller areas at one time.

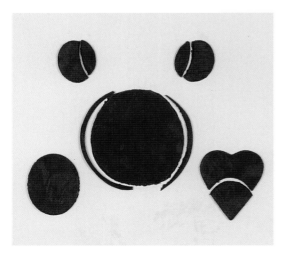

2 To make the head, place the round biscuit on a lined baking sheet then use the slightly larger 8.5cm (3³/₈") round cutter to remove a small crescent of dough from either side as shown. Use the same cutter to remove a section from the two smallest ovals and press these to the side of the head for the ears.

3 To make the muzzle, place the heart biscuit on a lined baking sheet and cut off the bottom half using the larger of the two oval cutters. Fit the large oval biscuit into the cut area.

4 Create the head and muzzle shapes for all of the biscuits on the baking sheet; don't move the biscuits

once they have been fitted together. Bake the biscuits for 10–12 minutes following the recipe.

TUTOR TIP

If you do not have oval cutters you can slim down a round biscuit by trimming away the sides with a large, round cutter.

Making and colouring the icing

5 Beat all the cookie icing mix with 75ml (2½oz) of cooled, boiled water until it forms standing peaks (see page 17). Weigh out 60g (2oz) of piping icing into a separate bowl. Add 45ml (1½oz) of cooled, boiled water to the remainder of the icing to make run-out icing (see page 17).

6 Divide the thick piping icing in half. Colour one portion dark brown with Bulrush liquid food colour and leave the remainder white. Fit two small piping bags each with a no. 1.5 nozzle and half-fill with the dark brown and white icing.

7 Colour the run-out icing as follows: leave 1tbsp white, colour 2tbsp beige using a small amount of Nasturtium, divide the remainder in half and colour one mid-brown with Bulrush and the other dark black-brown with Bulrush and Black. Finally add a touch of the mid-brown icing into the beige to tone down the brightness slightly.

Decorating the biscuits

8 Position the muzzle biscuit onto the head biscuit and draw around it with a black food colour pen to mark out the face; this area of the head biscuit will not be coated.

9 Use the food pen to mark the position of the eyes and other key features such as the nostrils. Although some of the facial features will be covered with icing it is useful to have a reminder of where to position the details.

10 Use the thick white piping icing to pipe over-sized pearls for the eyes.

11 Use the thick dark brown piping icing to outline the head and muzzle biscuits.

12 Fill two icing bottles or medium piping bags fitted with no. 2 nozzles with the mid-brown and black-brown run-out icings. Half-fill small piping bags with the beige and black run-out icings and cut a very small hole in the end of each bag.

13 Pipe a wedge-shaped line of beige icing at the top of the ear, starting at the join with the head. Pipe a line underneath with the black-brown icing and then the mid-brown. Fill in the small area in the centre with

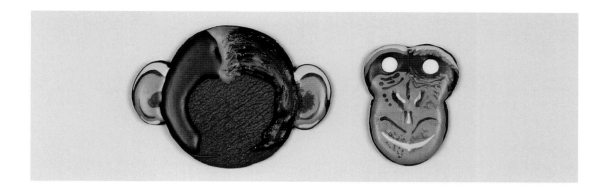

the black-brown icing, then add a couple of dots of black into the black-brown. Pull the black-brown icing into the mid-brown and blend the black dots into the surrounding black-brown icing. Repeat for the other ear.

14 Use the mid-brown run-out icing to pipe back-to-back C-shapes just off-centre down the forehead and fill in the triangular areas at the top and bottom of the C-shapes. Fill the rest of the forehead with the black-brown run-out icing then blend the colours by holding a scriber in the centre of the mid-brown and pulling into the darker brown following the curve of the head. Do not clean the scriber between strokes.

15 Fill down the sides of the head with black-brown run-out icing then add short lines of black, leaving the face area un-iced. Blend the colours using short, curved strokes with the scriber. Keep working the icing after the surface has started to dry to give a hairy texture. Set aside to dry.

16 Outline the very top of the heart with beige run-out icing, tapering to a point at the sides to create the brow. Add lines of mid-brown and black-brown underneath. Gently break the line between the beige and mid-brown using the scriber and pull the black-brown into the mid-brown.

17 Pipe black-brown around the eyes in the shape of an eye mask. Bring the mid-brown down to the nostrils. Immediately add lines of black-brown and black and blend them into the background icing.

18 Continue down the muzzle, forming the nostrils with black-brown and piping beige icing above for the nose. Add lines and dots and blend with a scriber to make the markings on the muzzle.

19 Pipe the mouth in beige run-out icing, tapering the ends and widening the centre of the lips. Create shadows above and below the mouth by blending in black-brown dots with the scriber. Once the muzzle biscuit is completely covered, set aside to dry.

20 Pipe a small amount of any icing onto the head and secure the muzzle on top.

21 Finish the chimpanzee by colouring in the eyes with a black food pen, leaving the base of the pearl white and adding a tiny dot of white run-out icing. Outline the eyes with the black food colour pen and define the nostrils and lips.

Tiger

EDIBLES

Vanilla biscuit dough (see recipe on pages 12–13)

500g (1lb 1¾oz) SK Art-Ice Cookie Icing Mix

SK Professional Liquid Food Colours: Berberis, Chestnut, Fern, Rose

SK Black Quality Food Colour (QFC) Dust

SK Black Food Colour Pen

EQUIPMENT

Essential equipment (see pages 8–9)

Cat face cookie cutter, approximately 9cm x 8.5cm (3½" x 3¼")

Piping nozzle: no. 1.5

Piping bottles or medium piping bags with no. 2 piping nozzles

Makes approx. 12 biscuits

Cutting out the biscuits

1 Prepare and roll out the vanilla biscuit dough following the recipe on pages 12–13. Cut out approximately 12 biscuits using the cat cutter then place on a lined baking tray and bake them for approximately 10–12 minutes. Allow to cool.

Making and colouring the icing

2 Beat all the cookie icing mix with 75ml (2½oz) of cooled, boiled water until it forms standing peaks (see page 17). Weigh out 60g (2oz) of piping icing into a separate bowl. Add 45ml (1½oz) of cooled, boiled water to the remainder of the icing to make run-out icing (see page 17).

3 Add Chestnut liquid food colour to the thick piping icing to make a light brown, similar to the biscuits. Fit a

small piping bag with a no. 1.5 nozzle into and half-fill with the light brown icing.

4 Divide and colour the run-out icing as follows: just under 1tbsp each coloured with Fern and Rose liquid colours, 2tbsp with black dust colour, and 250g (8¾oz) with a mixture of Chestnut and Berberis to make orange; leave the remaining icing white. Half-fill small piping bags with no nozzle with the Fern and Rose run-out icings and use icing bottles or medium piping bags fitted with no. 2 nozzles for the black, orange and white.

TUTOR TIP

The tiger biscuit is iced and patterned in one go with no drying time between the colours, so make sure you prepare all the piping bags or bottles before you start.

Decorating the biscuits

5 Use an orange food colour pen to sketch in the tiger's eyes, muzzle and guidelines for the black markings.

6 Use the light brown piping icing to outline the eyes and outer edge of the biscuits.

7 Start filling in the ears by piping a black line of run-out icing around the outside edge and a triangle at the base on the outside of each ear. Fill the main part of the ear with orange run-out icing and add white in the central area. Use the scriber to blend and pattern the ears.

8 Fill the forehead area with orange icing then add white eyebrows. Drop lines of black across the forehead then break the ends of the lines with the scriber. Pull the scriber through the centre of the black lines from between the eyes to the top of the head.

9 Bring the orange icing down around the eyes towards the muzzle, continuing to add markings with the white and black run-out icings as you work. Pipe a pink V for the nose and add a touch of white to highlight it. You can also add white icing between the nose and mouth on some of the tigers to create a little variation.

10 Pipe a thin line of white run-out icing from each side of the nose, down the centre and out to form the mouth. Fill in the space around the mouth with orange run-out icing then soften and shape the line with the scriber. Give the impression of whiskers by putting lines of white dots above the mouth, use virtually no pressure so the dots are tiny, then blend and shape with the scriber.

11 Pipe a narrow area of white icing at the sides of the face and chin, add patches of black and blend to form the markings. Fill in any uncovered areas around the cheeks and chin with orange then add further black markings under the eyes and around the muzzle before blending with the scriber.

12 Fill the lower part of the eyes with green run-out icing and add a circle of black at the top. Pipe in a tiny dot of white for a highlight. Once the biscuit is completely covered, set aside to dry fully.

13 Once the icing is completely dry, finish by outlining the eyes with a black food colour pen to give definition.

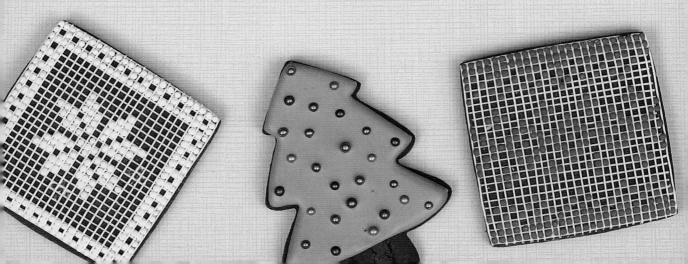

Festive Fun

Oh, Christmas Tree

EDIBLES

Chocolate biscuit dough (see recipe on pages 12–13)

1 egg, beaten

500g (1lb 1¾oz) SK Art-Ice Cookie Icing Mix

SK Dark Green Quality Food Colour (QFC) Liquid

SK Dark Green Quality Food Colour (QFC) Dust

SK Food Colour Pen (any colour)

SK Metallic Ball Dragées

Small amount of sugarpaste or marzipan (optional, for display)

EQUIPMENT

Essential equipment (see pages 8–9)

SK Christmas Tree Cookie Cutter

12 flat wooden lollipop sticks

Piping nozzle: no. 2

Tweezers

Small terracotta pots and granulated sugar (for display)

◆ ◆ ◆ ◆ ◆

Makes approx. 12 trees

Cutting out the biscuits

1 Draw a line 6cm (2³⁄₈") from one end of each lollipop stick with a food colour pen. Paint a little beaten egg along this 6cm (2³⁄₈") length with a pastry brush then space out the sticks on a lined baking sheet with the egg-covered side up.

2 Prepare and roll out the chocolate biscuit dough following the recipe on pages 12–13. Cut out the Christmas tree shapes and place one on top of each lollipop stick so that the base of the tree just covers the line. Press gently to attach the biscuit to the stick.

3 Bake the biscuits for 10–12 minutes following the recipe. Allow to cool.

Making and colouring the icing

4 Beat all the cookie icing mix with 75ml (2½oz) of cooled, boiled water until it forms standing peaks (see page 17). Before adding the additional water, colour the icing with the dark green liquid and dust colours and allow to stand as per the instructions.

5 Weigh out 60g (2oz) of the dark green piping icing into a separate bowl then add 45ml (1½oz) of cooled,

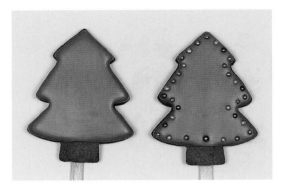

boiled water to the remainder of the icing to make run-out icing (see page 17).

Decorating the biscuits

6 Tip some of the dragées into the lid of the pot.

7 Fit a small piping bag with a no. 2 nozzle and half-fill with the thick piping icing. Outline the trees, leaving the trunk un-iced.

8 Carefully pour the thin run-out icing into an icing bottle and attach the nozzle. Fill the first tree, starting just inside the outline and working towards the centre.

9 As soon as you have iced the tree, use tweezers to drop dragées into the wet icing. Set aside to dry then repeat on each biscuit in turn.

TUTOR TIP

Follow the pictures as a guide or create your own individual designs with the dragées.

Finishing the biscuits

10 Fill some small pots with granulated sugar and push the trees into the sugar to resemble snow. If the trees are top-heavy, half-fill the pots with sugarpaste or marzipan to hold the sticks firmly then sprinkle some sugar on top.

TUTOR TIP

If you would like to make these biscuits as gifts for your friends and family, make a whole forest of Christmas trees, place each one in a clear cellophane bag then tie with festive ribbon.

Christmas Puddings

EDIBLES

Light gingerbread dough (see recipe on page 14)

500g (1lb 1¾oz) SK Art-Ice Cookie Icing Mix

SK Professional Liquid Food Colours: Bulrush, Mint, Poinsettia

SK Professional Poinsettia Dust Food Colour

50g (1¾oz) demerara sugar

EQUIPMENT

Essential equipment (see pages 8–9)

SK Christmas Pudding Cookie Cutter

3cm (1⅛") long holly leaf cutter

Piping nozzles: nos. 1, 1.5, 2 x no. 2

Small pieces of food-grade sponge

Makes approx. 10 biscuits

TUTOR TIP

These Christmas puddings would make ideal place setting name tags – an additional treat for a special day. The holly leaf with the name on it is iced and added separately, giving an extra dimension to these puddings.

Cutting out the biscuits

1 Prepare and roll out the gingerbread dough following the recipe on page 14. Cut out around 10 pudding biscuits and at least one additional holly leaf biscuit for each pudding. Place the holly leaves in the centre of the lined baking sheets with the puddings around the edge.

2 Bake the biscuits for approximately 10–12 minutes then allow to cool.

TUTOR TIP

If you have any spare biscuit dough, cut out extra holly leaves to practise writing the names on.

Making and colouring the icing

3 Beat all the cookie icing mix with 75ml (2½oz) of cooled, boiled water until it forms standing peaks (see page 17). Weigh out 60g (2oz) of piping icing into a separate bowl. Add 45ml (1½oz) of cooled, boiled water to the remainder of the icing to make run-out icing (see page 17).

4 Divide the thick piping icing in half. Colour one bowl of icing dark brown using Bulrush liquid food colour and the other using a combination of Poinsettia liquid and dust colours to achieve a bright red.

5 Colour the run-out icing with liquid food colours as follows: 1tbsp with Bulrush to make a very dark brown, 2tbsp with Mint to make a bright green, then divide the remainder in half, leave half white and colour the other half mid-brown using Bulrush.

Decorating the biscuits

6 Fit a small piping bag with a no. 1.5 nozzle and half-fill with the dark brown piping icing.

7 Half-fill a small piping bag with dark brown run-out icing and another with green run-out icing.

8 Using either piping bottles or medium piping bags with no. 2 nozzles, fill with the white and mid-brown run-out icings.

9 Draw a wavy line across the centre of the pudding and the outline of the two holly leaves with a food colour pen.

10 Use the bag of dark brown piping icing to pipe over the wavy line and outline the holly leaves and pudding.

11 Fill the lower half of the pudding with the mid-brown run-out icing and immediately drop in dots of dark brown run-out icing.

12 Place the biscuit on a piece of kitchen paper and thickly sprinkle over the demerara sugar. Quickly tip the biscuit upside down to allow the loose sugar to fall off.

13 Fill in the loose and pudding holly leaves with green run-out icing and use a slightly damp paintbrush to pull the icing into the points of the leaves where necessary. Set aside to dry for 10 minutes or so.

14 Fill in the top half of the biscuit with white run-out icing. Repeat to cover all of the puddings and leaves and allow the biscuits to dry completely.

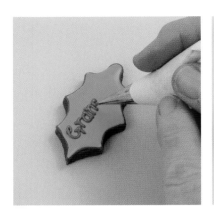  

Personalised holly leaves

15 Give the thick red piping icing a stir, then thin it slightly by rubbing down/paddling on the work surface (see page 120). Fit a small piping bag with a no. 1 nozzle and half-fill with the red icing. Use the piping bag like a pencil to write the name on the loose holly leaf biscuit, keeping the nozzle tip in contact with the icing. Make a personalised leaf for each recipient then allow to dry. Reserve the remaining red icing to pipe the berries later.

16 Place a small piece of food-grade sponge on the tip of the left-hand holly leaf on the pudding biscuit. Pipe a large blob of icing on the base of the personalised leaf and gently push it into place with the tip resting on the sponge. Allow the icing to firm up for 10 minutes or so.

17 Pipe holly berries onto the leaves and top of the pudding with the thick red icing to finish.

TUTOR TIP

If you are not very confident at piping directly onto the leaf biscuit, use a food colour pen to write on the biscuit first.

TUTOR TIP

To make a 3D version of these biscuits, cut out a 3.5cm (1⅜") square biscuit for every two puddings, cut in half diagonally and bake with the other biscuits. Fix a triangle biscuit to the back of the decorated puddings with a line of thick, brown piping icing so that it stands up like a picture frame.

Christmas Cross-stitch

EDIBLES

Vanilla or chocolate biscuit dough (see recipes on pages 12–13)

250g (8¾oz) SK White Professional Instant Mix Royal Icing

SK Professional Liquid Food Colours: Holly/Ivy, Leaf Green, Poinsettia

SK Poinsettia Professional Dust Food Colour

EQUIPMENT

Essential equipment (see pages 8–9)

8cm (3¹⁄₈") square biscuit cutter

Piping nozzles: 3 x no. 1

Templates (see page 124–125)

Makes approx. 10–12 biscuits

Cutting out the biscuits

1 Prepare and roll out the biscuit dough following the recipe on pages 12–13. When rolling out the biscuit dough try to keep it in an oblong shape to get as many biscuits as possible. Cut out the biscuits using an 8cm (3^1/$_8$") square cutter and place on a lined baking tray, ensuring there is plenty of space around them.

2 Chill the dough again after the biscuits have been cut out so that they hold their shape, then bake for approximately 10–12 minutes. Allow to cool.

TUTOR TIP

The chocolate dough is less liable to spread compared to the vanilla dough. If the biscuits come out of the oven with very bowed sides they can be straightened up when cold by gently grating off the rounded edges. Brush all crumbs away with a pastry brush before you start to decorate them.

Making and colouring the icing

3 Weigh and sift 250g (8¾oz) of royal icing mix into the bowl of a stand mixer. Add 35ml (1¼fl oz) of cooled, boiled water. Mix on the slowest speed with the flat beater until the icing forms standing peaks (see page 17).

4 Weigh out 60g (2oz) of icing into each of two bowls. Colour one with a mixture of Holly/Ivy and Leaf Green liquid food colours and the other with the Poinsettia liquid and dust colours to make a bright red. Leave the remainder of the icing white.

Decorating the biscuits

5 Fit a small piping bag with a no. 1 nozzle and half-fill with white icing.

6 Pipe a series of 26 parallel lines across the biscuit, starting and finishing at the very edge.

TUTOR TIP

To keep the lines straight and evenly spaced it can help to place the biscuit on a piece of squared paper. Draw over every other line on the paper with a red pen to make it easier to match each line top to bottom.

7 Turn the biscuit 90° and repeat step 6. Once you have finished piping the lines, mark the central square with a tiny dot of icing by counting 13 across and up.

8 The patterns are created by piping a tiny dot of either white or coloured icing in each square but in order to create a smooth surface, you will need paddle the icing on a work surface first to eliminate some of the air.

TOP TECHNIQUE

To paddle or rub down icing, place a small amount of icing in the colour required on a clean work surface and work the back of a palette knife backwards and forwards over the icing, keeping the blade of the knife in contact with the icing at all times. To test the icing, pull a peak up with the palette knife: the tip should fall over, not stand upright. If the icing is still stiff after paddling add one or two drops of cooled, boiled water.

9 Fit a small piping bag with a no. 1 nozzle and half-fill with paddled icing.

10 Find the central marked square and pipe the first dot in the pattern. Count out the number of dots to be piped to both the left and right of this dot.

11 Continue filling in the pattern by counting the dots on the templates. One you have completed the central design, pipe dots in various patterns to form the border.

TUTOR TIPS

- Before the dots are added to the designs the piped lines are very fragile. If you need to make manoeuvring the biscuit easier, fill in the outer-most squares first.

- If the icing has been standing for a while, quickly re-beat it before filling the piping bags.

- If you make a mistake it can be rectified by scooping out the icing while it is still wet with the point of a slightly damp paintbrush.

- For more pattern ideas, research cross-stitch and knitting books as well as the internet for different designs, such as letters and flowers. Remember the biscuits are small so keep it simple to fit within a 25 x 25 grid.

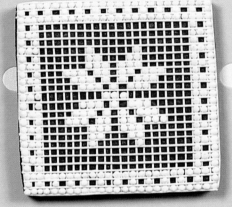

Templates

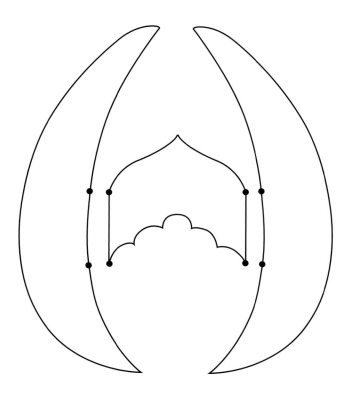

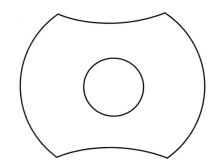

Pool Balls, pages 74–76

Fabergé Egg Biscuits, pages 68–72

Compass Biscuits, pages 77–79

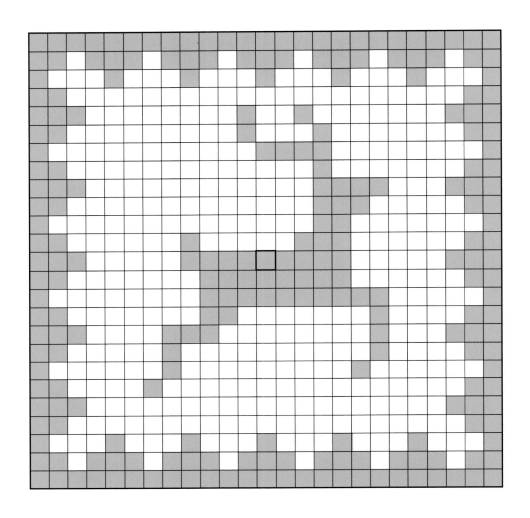

Christmas Cross-stitch, pages 119–122

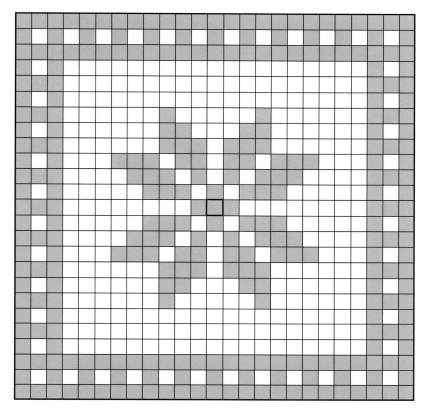

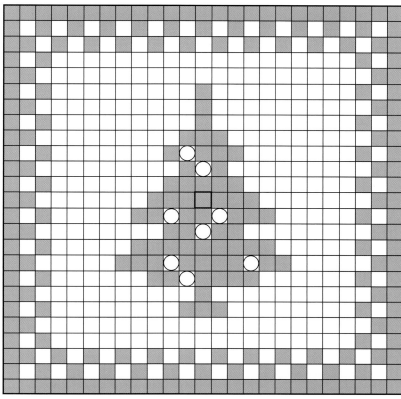

COME AND LEARN WITH US AT

SQUIRES KITCHEN™
INTERNATIONAL SCHOOL
the confidence to create

Squires Kitchen International School has been teaching the art of cake decorating and sugarcraft since 1987 and is now the leading independent school of its kind in the UK. From the basics of beautiful baking to mastering the art of cake decorating, chocolate and sugarcraft, Squires Kitchen gives its students the confidence to create.

Classes are taught at The Grange, a stunning Georgian style building in Farnham. Alongside cake decorating and sugarcraft courses, the cookery school boasts a fully equipped room complete with state-of-the-art appliances from Smeg. Students from all over the world learn from leading names in the industry who share their expert knowledge and experience, giving them the skills and confidence to take their interest to the next level.

Squires Kitchen International School works with a growing list of experts and professionals,

including leading sugarcrafters, master chocolatiers, celebrity chefs and professional bakers, meaning students can learn from the very best in the business. Our tutors are approachable and friendly and by maintaining small class numbers (12 maximum) this enables us to provide personable and intimate lessons focused on teaching techniques, answering questions and developing confidence.

The school is proud to be a member of the Independent Cookery Schools Association, the only accrediting body in the UK promoting excellence in cookery skills and training. We ensure our curriculum is always dynamic, modern and trend-setting and we provide classes for every level of ability, from Foundation to Masterclass. Our course and project range is always growing and changing with many options for home decorators, professional chefs and businesses alike.

Squires Kitchen International School is set apart from other cake decorating schools by our strong focus on nurturing and encouraging individual creativity; we believe this is the essence of being a successful baker or sugarcrafter. Alongside the technical skills, we provide the opportunity and environment for true vision and talent to flourish.

Find out more at www.squires-school.co.uk.

🐦 @SquiresSchool   f @SquiresKitchenSchool

★ 2016 ★
INDEPENDENT
COOKERY
SCHOOLS
ASSOCIATION

Squires Kitchen, UK
Squires House
3 Waverley Lane
Farnham
Surrey
GU9 8BB
0845 61 71 810
+44 (0) 1252 260 260
www.squires-shop.com

Squires Kitchen International School, UK
The Grange
Hones Yard
Farnham
Surrey
GU9 8BB
0845 61 71 810
+44 (0) 1252 260 260
www.squires-school.co.uk

For your nearest sugarcraft supplier, please contact customer@squires-shop.com.

  B. Dutton Publishing is an award-winning publisher of cake decorating titles.
To find out more about our books, follow us at
www.facebook.com/bduttonpublishing and **www.twitter.com/bduttonbooks**.

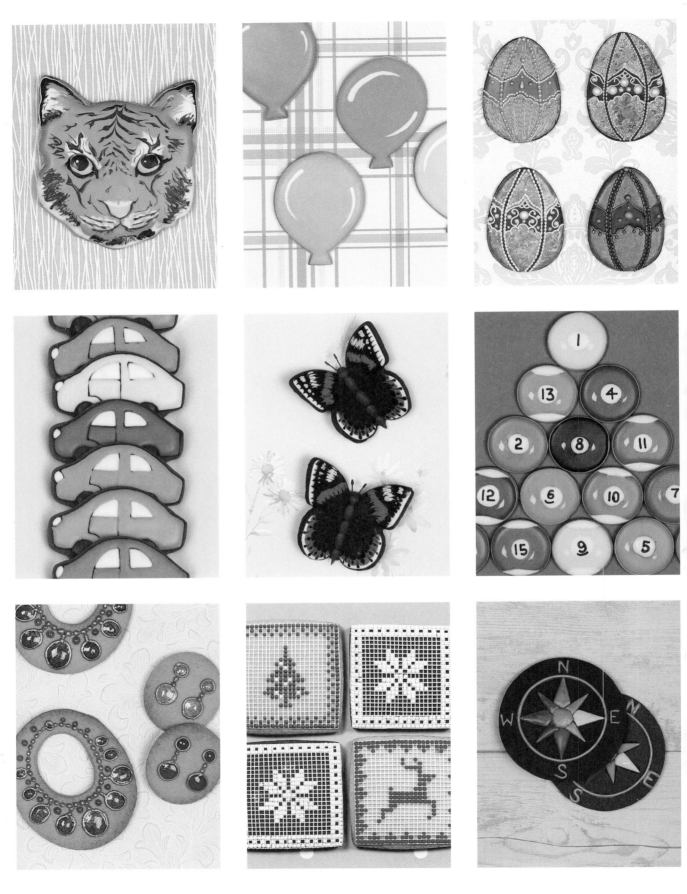